No Longer Lonely

A GAY FORMER PRIEST JOURNEYS

FROM HIS SECRET TO FREEDOM

Ray Buteau

BALBOA.
PRESS

A DIVISION OF HAY HOUSE

Balboa Press books may be ordered through booksellers or by contacting:

Balboa Press
A Division of Hay House
1663 Liberty Drive
Bloomington, IN 47403
www.balboapress.com
1-(877) 407-4847

Because of the dynamic nature of the Internet, any web addresses or
links contained in this book may have changed since publication and may
no longer be valid. The views expressed in this work are solely those
of the author and do not necessarily reflect the views of the publisher,
and the publisher hereby disclaims any responsibility for them.

The author of this book does not dispense medical advice or
prescribe the use of any technique as a form of treatment for physical,
emotional, or medical problems without the advice of a physician,
either directly or indirectly. The intent of the author is only to offer
information of a general nature to help you in your quest for emotional
and spiritual well-being. In the event you use any of the information
in this book for yourself, which is your constitutional right, the author
and the publisher assume no responsibility for your actions.

Any people depicted in stock imagery provided by Thinkstock are
models, and such images are being used for illustrative purposes only.
Certain stock imagery © Thinkstock.

ISBN: 978-1-4525-4435-9 (sc)
ISBN: 978-1-4525-4434-2 (e)

Print information available on the last page.

Balboa Press rev. date: 04/23/2015

NO LONGER LONELY

A former Roman Catholic priest reveals the cost of a lifetime of keeping his sexual orientation secret, his struggles with the church, his changing concept of God, and his finally arriving at a place of peace.

No Longer Lonely

"To isolate oneself is not to be at peace... Peace does not reject our longings, it is warm, not cold — a passionate commitment to becoming a full person. This means sacrificing the tidy goals of the fantasy person, one of which is that it is possible to live fruitfully in hostile isolation from our fellows."

Carel Weight, *The Silence*

DEDICATION

To my parents Leopold and Philippine
To my sisters Carole and Denise,
And to my brother Gaetan.

Acknowledgments

*"Many people other than the author contribute to
the making of a book, from the first person who had the
bright idea of alphabetic writing, through the inventor
of movable type to the lumberjacks who felled the trees
that were pulped for its printing. It is not customary
to acknowledge the trees themselves, though their
commitment is total."*
— Forsyth and Rada, Machine Learning

I want to acknowledge all the beautiful people who have
been a part of my spiritual journey and thus, have played
an integral part in the ultimate creation of this book:

- Those for whom reconciliation may not be
  possible but to whom I am grateful for the
  life lessons that I have received from having
  known you.
- Those I have considered as mentors among
  the Christian clergy, my doctors and spiritual
  directors, and my mentors in the gay
  community.

- Darren, who guided me in the initial editing, restructuring and formatting of my previous manuscript.
- My niece Jacinta, for her time in computer support and photography.
- The writers-in-residence who have guided me, and those who proofread my final copy, for their input and encouragement.
- Rick Johnson who respectfully edited this book
- To all who have helped me articulate my thoughts into words

As I began to understand my experiences, I thought of my life as a human tragedy, but today I see it, as the make-up of my human and spiritual journey, as a grace from God.

To each of you, Namaste.

"Life is a gathering of experiences."
— *Joseph P. Cambell*

Contents

FOREWORD

*"Know that the purpose for which each soul enters a
material experience is that it may be a light unto others."*
Edgar Cayce

One's sexual orientation was not discussed in good
Catholic families in the 1960s and 70s. It was not discussed
in elementary school or high school, and certainly not in
Catholic seminary or amongst straight, ordained priests
or with parishioners. Yet, sexuality is always a big issue,
particularly amongst adolescents, and especially amongst
the precocious youth of that era.

In "proper" families, sexual orientation, particularly
if you were not "straight," was so beyond "big issue" that
it was best kept secret... like a personal fault or shameful
character flaw.

When added to my feelings of isolation and loneliness
in keeping my secret, the expectations of parishioners
and of the church hierarchy left me feeling trapped and
helpless, so it was not surprising that my spirit was at a
point of burnout in 1991 when I asked for a year off. In

the past, my spiritual directors and councillors had all asked me to journal; during that break, I discovered a strong need to do so. As Steven Berkoff said, "Writing is an antidote for loneliness."

Along with attending a workshop by Patrick O'Leary SJ, one of the co-authors of *The Enneagram, a Journey of Self Discovery,* I journaled my experiences and found myself becoming addicted to using the one skill I did manage to retain from high school besides dancing — typing. Like a savoury, medium well-done steak, I devoured Michael H. Crosby's book *The Dysfunctional Church,* which deals with the power and control of the church institution. Time ceased, meals became irregular, walks in the park became more frequent, and pages upon pages of writing on every aspect of my life — my studies, ministry, concerns, and hopes — became words before my very eyes. As I accumulated folders on dozens of topics I began realizing I could write a book.

As my printouts piled up, I also read Reginald W. Bibby's book, *Unknown Gods, the Ongoing Story of Religion in Canada.* It fuelled my writing and, at the end of the year, I titled my manuscript *Responding in Silence.*

In 1994, after reading Alice Miller's book *The Drama of the Gifted Child* and Pat Collins' CM work, *Intimacy and the Hungers of the Heart,* and as I dealt with issues of guilt, shame, blaming, and feelings of co-dependency with the Catholic institution, I reworked the manuscript. It was also at that time that I was moved by the movie *The Priest* and the play *Liar.*

As I began my ministry in chaplaincy in 1997, the manuscript was reworked again after I read Richard J.

Gilmartin's *Pursuing Wellness, Finding Spirituality,* and Diarmuid O'Murchu's book *Reclaiming Spirituality.* I was moving to spirituality beyond religiosity.

In 2002, the church institution used homosexuality as a scapegoat — as referred to in *2002, Betrayal,* on the crisis in the Catholic Church. After attending a workshop by Lisa McGifford on domestic abuse that year, my manuscript was reworked yet again, based on the cycle of abuse, and was renamed *Behind the Smile.*

In 2006, an acquaintance introduced me to the writings of Andrew Tobias, *The Best Little Boy in the World.* The acquaintance helped me, in his words, to minimize as much mumbo jumbo and psycho babble as possible" from the manuscript and to concentrate on three main points: my being gay, my relationships with others, and my relationship with God. At the time, I was trying to articulate my isolation, coming out as a gay person, owning my truth, and the price to be paid for doing so.

During that time, I was also influenced by the writings of Louise L. Hay, *You Can Heal Your Life;* Dr. Wayne W. Dyer, *The Power of Intention;* Eckhart Tolle, *A New Earth,* and by the DVD *What the Bleep? Down the Rabbit Hole,* dealing with quantum physics. At the end of 2008, the title of my manuscript was changed to *My Secret With God.*

Secrets can be dangerous. My secret, maintained throughout a lifetime, could be deadly. Like many of my generation, and many more even today, I struggled with it, and its fallout in serious emotional challenges, lifestyle dilemmas, and impossible spiritual peace. As a Catholic priest, I thought I would find refuge, a hiding place from the expectations of a heterosexual culture, yet the promise of celibacy and the loneliness that are built into the church only magnified all the usual difficulties and condemned me to a life alone, outside the mainstream community.

How does one reconcile with what is deemed by many to be a culturally and religiously unacceptable sexual orientation? How does one find peace within such a dilemma?

From September to April, 2009, I compiled all the work I had done from 2006 to 2008, making it more personal, owning my truth and speaking more about the process of moving on. The new manuscript was entitled *Going Beyond Reconciliation*.

In October, 2009, a local library writer in residence suggested I hire an editor to reorganize my manuscript. Finally, in April 2010, the manuscript was edited and, nineteen years after it began, the book became No Longer Alone.

Though 'alone', I was feeling confident and enjoying my independence as the months passed quickly, sharing my manuscript and praying daily to be guided to the right literary agent. Then on April 26th 2011 while listening to an insightful web-cast on transformation, it became clearer to me that my book — which is about the sadness and pain in feeling lonely in my relationship with the Church because of having to keep my secret, - needed a title to reflect my present experience of being no longer lonely, as I no longer needed to keep my secret.

I believe my perspective on maintaining a healthy balance within ourselves, between ourselves, and with our higher power can offer peace, spiritual wholeness, and hope for a fulfilling and contented life. My hope is that my story will offer to others a way of maintaining health, whether they are facing the same or similar challenges that come from being gay, or some other of life's spiritually and emotionally difficult times.

Yet it is in this loneliness that the deepest activities begin.
It is here that you discover act without motion, labour
that is profound repose, vision in obscurity, and, beyond
all desire, a fulfillment whose limits extend to infinity.
Thomas Merton, a 20th century Trappist monk

Ray Buteau

Introduction

The 'Outing' — Part 1

*H*eadingley Correctional Centre is a few miles west of Winnipeg. The kilometre or so drive down the scenic and serene road off the Trans Canada Highway is a stark contrast to life inside the institution's walls. In summer, it is lined with trees and well-cut lawns, often rabbits and deer graze within easy sight. I frequently slowed down to let them pass. In winter, the sun sparkles off a blanket of snow that pretty much covers everything as far as the eye can see.

On that traumatic day of my life, the drive in from the highway was remarkably still and silent. As the car approached the checkpoint halfway between the highway and the centre, the duty officer recognized me as a staff member, nodded, and waved me through. Once parked, I plugged in the car, hung my parking pass on the rear view mirror, locked up, and walked toward the front door.

A white limousine was parked there and I thought at first that someone special must be visiting. But then the prison doors opened and an inmate, a gang member, walked out and headed for the limo. With a lot of the other inmates watching, he climbed in and it drove off. The practice, while certainly popular with the inmates, has since been stopped.

I buzzed the front door and waited to be identified via an overhead camera. The cameras were everywhere, constantly observing everyone. A loud buzz let me through the first door but I had to wait a few seconds for the outside door to close before the next heavy steel door would open.

Instantly, I heard the clashing of steel doors, the sounds of officers shouting orders and the foul language from inmates as they passed one another in the halls. The strong smell of bacon grease greeted my arrival. Inmates were coming and going from the cafeteria with complaints about the food, the coffee, the amount they received or the little time they had to eat it. For every meal, every day, they had the same complaints, always with the same strong odour of grease as a backdrop.

Down the hallway, I stopped to sign in and greet the guards on duty.

"Good morning Father Ray," they always replied.

From there, I buzzed another set of barred doors and was let into the main hallway. Once inside, I tried to avoid colliding with the chaos — others coming and going, trays of food being brought to segregated areas, inmates in chains being escorted to court hearings, outside appointments or family funerals.

"Hey chaplain, I need to see you soon," someone shouted.

"Fill out a request form," I shouted back.

Two flights of stairs lead to the Spiritual Care Department with its four offices: one for an aboriginal elder; one for the chaplain, who is the department head; mine; and a spare office for interviews. There is also a chapel area that seats fifty, a classroom used by interns studying clinical pastoral education, and a lounge area where the chaplains meet.

I greeted my co-worker, Rev, and no sooner had I settled into my office and started going through my list of inmate requests when the phone rang. The call was from the newly appointed head of provincial chaplains.

"Good morning Ray," he said, "this is Mike... an urgent matter has come up and I need to come to the institution to speak to you about it."

"Oh... Okay," I said tentatively. "I'll be here... and look forward to meeting with you."

Bewildered, I shared the news with Rev, who seemed both surprised and uncomfortable. I asked him if he knew what it could be about and he said he had no idea. While we waited for Mike, Rev made some coffee and I went down to the cafeteria to see if I could get some pastries.

When Mike arrived, formalities were dealt with more quickly than usual; he seemed to be in a hurry to speak to me. I absentmindedly asked if Rev could join us, not realizing how personal the issue was, and Mike anxiously agreed to have Rev present.

"I'm sorry to inform you that a sexual accusation has been made against you, Ray," he blurted as soon as the door was shut. "I've notified the superintendent and your bishop."

I looked at Rev in shock and embarrassment, and wondered why he was allowed to witness my humiliation. I later discovered that everyone except me had already known the subject at hand.

"What's this all about?" I asked in total disbelief. I had never received any notification of an accusation and didn't know what he was talking about. When I learned that even the superintendent and my bishop had been notified before me, I was numb with disbelief.

Rev watched in silence as Mike asked me if I knew a certain inmate..

"Yes," I said, "I met with him after he arrived a few weeks ago."

I had been asked to see that particular inmate and, after speaking with him and hearing his story, he had looked at me and said, "You don't recognize me do you, Father Ray?"

"No, I'm sorry, I don't... have we met?"

He proceeded to describe my apartment in detail and the one-night stand we had had a few years before.

"I'm sorry if knowing who I am is a problem for you," I had said with a calmness that surprised even me. "Under the circumstances," I went on, "I need to notify my co-worker about this... it might be better for you to see him instead of me."

"I would feel more comfortable seeing you," he said, "since you know who I am and what I will have to deal with here."

"I'm willing to see you, but I need to notify my co-worker about the situation anyway."

Rev had been my supervisor during clinical training and I think he considered himself a friend. He knew me better than most and was always aware and supportive of my orientation, as long as it was not an issue for me in what could be a very dangerous environment. I assured him that it had not been an issue during my parish ministry, and was not an issue at the prison.

"So what do you want to do?" Rev had asked at the time.

"I know how he has to be and how difficult it will be for him in this environment. Even though we have obviously had a sexual encounter, I can honestly say I don't remember him, as horrible as that may sound, but that's not unusual for a one-night stand. He would like to continue seeing me while he's here but I don't know how you feel about that."

"I'll have a talk with him and let you know," he said, Later, Rev told me he thought Steve understood that I should not continue to meet with him for spiritual care.

"What am I being accused of?" I ask the provincial chaplain.

He explained in graphic detail an intense sexual encounter, which supposedly had been videotaped and, according to the chaplain as well, had gone on for a few days.

"I admit I probably had an encounter with this man because he knows my apartment in detail, but I deny having done any of those masochistic activities, or having a camera on, and I'm prepared to take a lie detector test to prove it."

But I was guilty by accusation; those in authority had been notified and my fate was sealed.

"You will have to see your bishop, who has been notified," the chaplain added. "You will not be able to keep your position here as chaplain without his endorsement and, of course, you need to speak to the superintendent as soon as possible, before this gets out into the institution."

I couldn't believe what was happening and what was being said. It all hit me hard! There had been no warning, only a complete disregard for normal protocol in dealing with sensitive personnel matters. And it was all stated in such a matter-of-fact, guilt-assumed way it took my breath away.

Then, with a curt, "Sorry about all this Ray... good luck to you," the provincial chaplain was out the door.

Rev looked agitated as he said he would be supportive and suggested I see the superintendent.

"Is this true Ray," JR asked?

"It's true that I probably did have a sexual encounter with the guy, though I don't remember him... but the details are false... I'm willing to take a lie detector test."

"Ray, I'll take your word for it," he said, "and I'll have the inmate transferred immediately, before things start being said... but what about your position here, we need an endorsement from your bishop for you to stay."

As I listened to him, still in disbelief, he went on. "I suggest you go and see him as soon as possible and report back to me. You need to deal with this as soon as possible."

And with that, my schedule for the next month took a drastic change.

The bishop, of course, was expecting my call. It was 2002; he was new to our diocese and not in the mood for anything remotely similar to the priest/pedophile scandals that were hitting the media at the time and could put him in the spotlight. He was direct, to say the least.

"Are you living a celibate life?"

"No Bishop, I am not,"

"Then you're to stop your lifestyle and live the chaste life you have been called to live, is that clear?"

"The only thing that isn't clear, Bishop, is whether I can live a celibate life. I'm questioning my calling to the priesthood."

"In that case, I'm sure you've heard of Southdown (a psychological treatment centre north of Toronto). I am sending you there for an evaluation and assessment of your ability to live a chaste, celibate life."

As he shook my hand goodbye, he added, "You will be contacted in a few days; be prepared to leave for a week's evaluation."

With a bishop, there is seldom a "choice" about whether you want to do something or not, only ultimatums.

The following day, I got a call telling me that I had a flight to Toronto on Sunday and would be picked up at the airport when I landed, the details were to be emailed shortly. I had two days to notify the superintendent and a few friends, and to get myself ready.

Sunday evening, I arrived in Toronto and headed for the airport exit to look for the white limo and chauffeur that were to be waiting for me.

1
Becoming

The Early Years

"The trees are God's great alphabet: With them He writes
in shining green
Across the world His thoughts serene."
— Leonora Speyer

"**W**here are you going to plant those trees Dad?"

"One is going in the front yard, and the other in the back."

Being only six years old, the eight-foot twigs looked very high when Dad stood them up; more like long poles than trees because they had few branches. The root ends were wrapped in sackcloth bags, which Dad left on them as he put them directly into the holes he had dug, then he untied the bags and filled in the holes with topsoil. We patted and stomped the earth around the base of the trunk to make sure it was solidly in place.

"Water those trees every day and they'll live and grow... don't, and they won't," he pronounced as he stood back to appreciate his efforts.

We watered them every day and waited for signs of life. Finally, buds appeared and opened, and in the fall, after the few leaves that had been produced that year had turned crimson and fell to the ground, Dad wrapped the branches in cloth to protect them through their first winter.

As spring approached, I checked those trees daily for signs of life. When they appeared in the form of small buds that seemed to double in size every day, I was amazed and felt a kinship to those scrawny trees. As the days and weeks passed, the buds grew, slowly opening into hundreds of leaves that covered every branch as it stretched out to do its part in forming a beautifully full red maple. I loved those trees from the day we planted them and felt peace just being near them. Dad said they were nice but really just reminded him of his second most favourite NHL hockey team and how poorly they were doing.

Unlike my dad, my male friends and I were not the least interested in hockey, or sports of any kind for that matter, though we did play a version of softball in the backyard on occasion. We preferred playing and trading marbles, making forts, wrestling around on the lawn, and just hanging out.

When I wrestled with another boy on the thick green grass of our lawn and held him down, or squeezed him in a headlock, his warmth, his scent and closeness felt good to me, even excited me, though I didn't understand why.

It often happened that when I had one of them in a good neck hold or was on top of him, Mom would shout at me, "Ray, it's time to come in now." And when Mom said "now," she meant, "NOW!"

She didn't seem to like my male friends. Though she never said so outright, she did ask a few times why I liked playing with them so much. Sensing that she didn't approve, I didn't have the courage to tell her that they made me feel good. She never stopped me from playing with female friends, even when we were in a tent made with blankets in the backyard, or alone in the basement. But with my female friends, I felt nothing special at all.

Perhaps Mom suspected something was amiss with me and other boys. Perhaps it was just that more of my male friends were not Catholics. According to her and my dad, unless my friends converted and became Roman Catholic before they died, they couldn't go to heaven. Even at six years old, I couldn't understand that because I really liked my male friends, and their parents. But my parents, along with the priests at church and the nuns at school, all believed it, so it had to be true.

Dad was particularly unshakeable. What the Pope said, God agreed with. And what Dad said about God, we believed, like "Water those trees every day and they'll live and grow, don't, and they won't." I could understand and believe that, so I thought his other "pronouncements" must be true too. Yet, deep down in my stomach, it didn't feel right that God would make my friends go to hell simply because they were not Catholic. It just didn't make sense to me.

But nothing was more important to my parents than being Roman Catholic. I remember a new high school was being built in our neighborhood but the Catholic high school, which my parents and the Catholic community expected me to attend, was in the southern part of the city and included an expensive tuition fee with uniforms. My parents weren't ready for the tuition and extra expenses so I got to attend the new high school in the opposite direction, in Protestant territory no less.

The school was a hot bed of activity and energy. It was the 1960s and the environment was exciting. Though shy and timid, my new male friends and I actually became the "in-crowd" and soon attracted female friends. They all lived in very nice homes and had things that I didn't, like their own bedrooms with their own radios, record players, records, magazines and posters on their walls.

Except for some of the major sports, we got involved in every school activity: the school choir, drama class, camera and social clubs, the curling team, the year book club, and were even elected to the student council.

The 60s were the time of the Beatles and Beatle mania, psychedelic music, Bob Dylan and Simon and Garfunkel. We danced the twist and the monkey. I loved dancing and had a natural sense of rhythm. Girls wore miniskirts and tall leather boots and the guys wore paisley shirts, bright, bold colours and tight, very tight, velvet trousers revealing every crack and bulge. And, of course, we all had long hair. The look was a mixture of oriental, African, space-age and hippie. We went to the movies a lot, seeing Psycho, Spartacus, Exodus and Where the Boys Are.

It was also the dawning of the age of television and we watched The Andy Griffith Show, Candid Camera, The Jack Benny Show, Denis the Menace, My Three Sons, The Ed Sullivan Show, Perry Mason, Bonanza, The Red Skelton Show, and Alfred Hitchcock Presents.

But, by the end of Grade 10, my parents were feeling a lot of pressure, via the regular Sunday announcements at church to all parents to send their children to the "right" school. I didn't like the idea of being separated from my friends but I knew that my parents actually believed my going to a Catholic school was important for me, so I did.

Religious education classes were more like health classes in which we studied what we couldn't and shouldn't do with our bodies. I soon began to understand another reason why my parents might have wanted me to go to that school — we would be talking about the one topic that they never talked about — sex! I quickly learned that sex and sin were closely related.

Religious education was taught by a teaching order of priests, the Holy Cross Fathers. These men were fun to talk to and very serious about their faith. One early class that immediately got everyone's attention began with the Father pronouncing: "Today we are going to speak about a very serious mortal sin, which we need to control in our lives."

"*Sounds interesting,*" I thought as I, and everyone else in the class, fixed their eyes on him.

"And that's masturbation," he continued.

Masturbation was a normal part of our development, he admitted, but also a mortal sin! It was not meant for our carnal pleasure; it had to be controlled and should be confessed. Other guys chuckled as the priest spoke, but not me. My heart rate quickened and I could feel my face flush as I realized I had frequently been committing a mortal sin and didn't even know it. I don't think I heard anything else the priest said in that class.

That year, though I was no longer wrestling with my male friends, I felt even more attracted to them. I was surrounded by guys in tight jeans and, even when they wore blazers, their front bulge was obvious. I didn't understand why I felt the way I did. In those days we never spoke about gays; I didn't know anything about homosexuality. I thought my sexual attraction to men was something peculiar only to me; I didn't know why I thought and felt the way I did. I was just terrified of what might happen to me if someone found out.

I tried praying the thoughts away, but that only stalled the inevitable because my imagination would be re-activated the second I came across a guy who was well built — not to mention the effect gym classes had on me. I had to be very careful not to be caught looking below the belt. So I fantasized, masturbated, and went to confession.

Actor Steve McQueen became a kind of fantasy lover. Seeing him in movies or magazines always aroused me to masturbate. I didn't know why, but I knew it was a serious mortal sin. I felt there was something very wrong with me. I was afraid if my mother found out she would send me away somewhere to "get treated". I thought of speaking to one of the priests about it but feared he would need to tell my parents, or worse, try to get me to tell them myself.

As it was, any communication with my mother was difficult at best. And when she was angry or, for some reason, annoyed with me about something, she would go off to her ironing, or sewing, or read her newspaper rather than talk with me about whatever it was.

"Mom, what's the matter?" I would ask, and she would quickly put her hand out towards me, motioning me to stop.

"I don't want to talk about it," she would say.

I always knew I had hurt her feelings when she gave me that silent, glaring look that seemed to go right through me. Other times, when I wanted to go out somewhere, she would ask, "Why are you always going out? Why don't you stay home once in awhile?"

And if I was relaxing at home, watching TV or reading, she would ask, "Why don't you go and visit someone instead of just sitting around all the time?"

Staying in Mom's good favour meant doing the dishes without being asked and taking care of my brother and sisters. To her credit, when I was younger she had tried to get me interested in the accordion, which I could hardly hold, but then she did get me into tap dancing, which I excelled at. The music, the satin, studded costumes, the makeup, the lights, the applause; it all excited me.

My parents, and even my friends, could tell something was bothering me in those latter high school days.

"What's the matter Ray?" Mom would ask, and I would echo back, "It's nothing, I don't want to talk about it." That was usually the limit of conversations with Mom, but not with God.

The thought that masturbation, which felt normal and pleasurable to me, was somehow displeasing to God just didn't make sense. I had always thought of myself as a good and caring person and wasn't trying to disobey Him, or anyone. I just could not accept that God was unconditional love and at the same time would judge me and condemn me to hell for this "mortal sin". Why would God even care if I masturbated? Was the church telling God what was right and wrong? Was God just going along with what the church was teaching us? If I didn't confess my mortal sin and died, would God go along with what they were saying and condemn me to eternity in hell?

Everyone was telling me that that was what our faith taught and what God was asking of me. Increasingly, I felt I was left with no choices.

One day, on my knees in the school chapel, I said to God, "In my heart I know what I'm being taught is not right, and that I won't be condemned for what I am doing. I will continue to confess it, just in case, but I know that if I die I am not going to hell."

God kept my secret.

Later that year, I was persuaded to take part in a school skit for a fundraising event.

"Sure, why not," I responded without question, not realizing I would be playing the part of one of our school teachers, a priest. My parents didn't know what role I had. I asked them one day if they would tell me how my costume looked and see if it needed any alterations. They agreed, and I got dressed. As I came out of the bedroom looking like a Holy Cross Father, they gasped.

"Wait a minute!" Mom exclaimed as she quickly went for the camera. The "seed" had been planted.

After that year, I wanted out of the Catholic school and to go back to being with my friends at the regular high school. My parents saw that I had really been struggling with my grades and would have to take summer classes to be accepted into Grade 12, so they agreed to the change.

Back with my friends at Lakeport with all its new facilities, including a large gymnasium that was perfect for school dances, I noticed quite a change in the guys. They were forever talking about girls and wanting parties so they could have those slow, close, cheek-to-cheek, body to-body dances. I much preferred to rock and roll.

To add fuel to the fire, we decided that when there wasn't a school dance we would take turns hosting a weekend dance party at each other's homes. All we needed were balloons, streamers, coke, chips, a full punch bowl, a record player, lots of records and a volunteer to keep them playing. We notified all of our neighbours and invited their kids if they were our age and told everyone when the party would end. My parents liked our group and would welcome us. In fact, if Mom hadn't nudged Dad to leave, on many occasions he probably would have stayed the whole evening to talk to everyone.

There was one girl that I liked as a friend and as a great dance partner. I felt safe and comfortable with Cathy because I didn't feel I had to do anything intimate with her. She didn't seem to like the slow dances either. Though we did them, neither of us got excited by them. We both loved dancing and we needed room to move when we rock-and-rolled, danced the cha-cha, the polka and the twist. The "monkey" didn't require much room at all. Cathy wasn't any more romantically interested in me than I was in her so we got along well.

In fact, no one in the group seemed interested in dating or going steady, but the guys were interested in getting laid and tried to get me to go along with them on their bar pick-ups. I always had an excuse for not being available — usually some Catholic event. I just wasn't interested in girls in the same way they were, but I couldn't tell them that. They would want to know why and if I told them I'd lose them as friends. Trying to avoid the topic and the invitations to go out with them became very tiring.

More and more, my secret restricted my social life as the months went by. I tried to focus on my homework but as the year progressed, the pressures continued to build. My friends wondered why I wasn't joining in and I couldn't tell them why I wasn't interested, all of which made me wonder what I was going to do with my life, how I was going to keep my secret, what kind of career I wanted, or could have. And still, I visited the confessional booth all too often. Something had to give.

The Call

"The primal call is the call to love. It is a call to be loving and to accept love in return. It calls us beyond rhetoric and beyond excuses. It calls us out of ourselves."
— David Spangler, The Call

Every year, as sure as buds reappear on the trees, a Catholic Sunday service is set aside in which all priests speak from the pulpit to encourage young men to think of a vocation in the priesthood. One particular "Vocation Sunday", I was forced to begin opening up like the buds when our newly ordained priest asked the question, "Have you ever thought of the priesthood?"

I hadn't... and he seemed to be speaking directly to me. I had never thought about giving my life to God. After all that God had done for me, I had never considered devoting my life to His service and felt tremendous guilt. The notion felt right, like God was guiding me, giving me a way out. As a priest I wouldn't have to worry about my sexual feelings, I would receive a good education, and my friends and family would respect my choice of career. I was overcome with emotion.

It felt as if someone had just asked me a very important question, which they had, but I didn't know how to answer it. Why was I feeling close to tears? I was 20 years old, confused about my attraction to other men, unable to see myself settling down with a woman, and I had no one to speak to about any of it.

When I arrived home that day, I saw the *Annals of St. Anne de Beaupre* on the living room coffee table alongside my mother's newspaper. I picked it up, sat on the couch, and began browsing through it when I noticed a picture of an old man in a light-tan, hooded garment, looking serene, intent in prayer.

"Mom, who is this man," I asked. "What's this about?"

"It's about Trappist Monks," she replied. "They're a cloistered order, spending their days in work and prayer and most of that in silence."

"How very different," I thought.

I was familiar with Buddhist Monks but hadn't known that the Catholic Church also had monks.

Without telling anyone, I sent away for information and, a couple of weeks later, received an envelope with large red letters written across the top — "Trappist Monks".

"Are you seriously thinking about becoming a monk?" my mother asked as I stared at the envelope.

"I just wanted to know more about it," I said. "Do you remember that sermon when Father asked, 'Have you ever thought of the priesthood'?" I asked.

The question immediately secured her undivided attention. "Well," I went on, "I have been thinking about it but I am not sure if I want to become a priest. I'm really bothered by how I feel and I don't know what to do about it."

Scarcely controlling her excitement, she said, "You should go and see the parish priest and talk to him about it."

I had to admit, choosing to become a monk seemed preferable to becoming a parish priest. I had always thought of parish priests as rather materialistic, living the good life with fancy cars, nice residences, and even housekeepers. I felt called to a closer relationship with God but didn't understand what that might involve.

As the weeks went by, more envelopes started arriving from different religious communities: Dominicans, Franciscans, White Fathers, Jesuits, Redemptorists, and many others.

Meanwhile, my grandmother Maillet didn't want to see me become a cloistered monk so she had my uncle send away for information from religious communities that offered seminary studies. One such community caught my attention, the Institute Voluntas Dei. Grandmother Maillet knew about it through the chaplain at her seniors' home and recommended it to me.

I was interested in their set-up. I'd be able to go to the seminary and try it for a year to see if the lifestyle was for me. Because it was funded by benefactors and not the Catholic Church, I wouldn't have to be affiliated with any bishop.

However, in spite of the information I had, I was confused and unsure about what I wanted to do. I felt I had to speak to the priest who had raised the question. I called to arrange to speak to him and went to the rectory a few days later. The young priest was very gracious, kind and supportive.

"I had never thought about having a closer relationship to God until you asked the question in your sermon," I told him.

"You seem quite troubled by this," he said, "and your emotions are, perhaps, a sign that God is calling you to the priesthood." That made some sense to me but I wasn't convinced.

"But I haven't taken any Latin," I said, which was a requirement for seminary entrance.

"I'm willing to teach you Latin during the summer months," he suggested, "and, along with a tutor, I'll prepare you for the entrance exams."

I was still not convinced but I said, "If you are willing to do all this for me, I'm willing to try it for a year."

That summer, the trees Dad and I had planted when I was six were over 15 feet high, with a diameter of branches and red maple leaves just as wide. They provided comfort and refreshing shade for me while I studied my *Living Latin* textbook. Under their branches I not only felt protected from the heat of the sun, but also connected to something much bigger than me, to something universal and spiritual — to God.

At the end of that summer, I applied to the institute and was accepted. At the time, I knew nothing about homosexuality, or about the notion of "coming out" and living life as a gay man. I thought keeping my secret was my means of survival. The life- changing sermon and grandma's intervention were, for me, God's intervention, guiding and protecting me. Like many similarly oriented men, I was marrying in order to further protect my secret. But unlike straight men who married, it would not be a woman with whom I would find shelter.

Minor Seminary

'Know thyself'
— Plato 427 BC-347 BC

𝓘 sat under the red maple tree in the back yard enjoying the warm summer evening. Thoughts of the day Dad and I had planted the tree so many years before triggered a flood of flashbacks of my childhood and teen years, of memories, good and bad, of times with Mom and Dad and my brother and sisters. A sad nostalgia battled with excitement about the future.

"People in suburbia see trees differently than foresters do. They cherish every one. It is useless to speak of the probability that a certain tree will die when the tree is in someone's backyard... You are talking about a personal asset, a friend, a monument, not about board feet of lumber."
— Roger Swain

I wanted to enjoy the setting sun and the sound of the gentle breeze rustling through the leaves above me, but in the morning my parents were taking me to the bus depot and I knew I should go in and spend a little time with them before finishing my last-minute packing and heading for bed.

The next morning, as the bus pulled away, at first my eyes stung with insistent tears but it wasn't long before my mind dwelt less on the chapter of life I was closing and more on anticipation of the one I was opening. Before I knew it, we had arrived at the Institute Voluntas Dei Seminary in Trois Rivieres, Quebec and the pace quickened as I began the registration process.

My first surprise came quickly with news that I would have a roommate. Surprise Number 2 was being introduced to him right then and there. Pierre looked very pleasant, indeed! The priest introduced us and asked him to show me to our room and help me settle in before supper.

As we made our way through the organized confusion, he introduced me to students from all over the world. I was surprised to meet fellow seminarians from Sri Lanka, Trinidad, France, Laos and Haiti. The fraternity was striking, invigorating, as if everyone had known each other for years.

"All first and second-year students are bunked together," Pierre said as we finally approached the dormitory. "Third-year students have their own rooms."

Our room had all the basics — two beds, desks, bookshelves, dressers and — Pierre! When it was time to call it a day, he had no problem taking off his clothes in front of me and lying on his bed in his underwear. He was six feet tall and muscular, with broad shoulders, a nice chest, strong arms and legs, and a nice butt. His light hair was thick and his eyes brown — definitely a good looking young man to say the least; not a model, but close and, yes, I definitely noticed.

But I wasn't ready for him! Until that first night with Pierre, I had had my fantasies about Steve McQueen, but here I was, my first night in the seminary with this six-foot, good looking man laying before me in his underwear. I had a difficult time maintaining eye contact.

I put on my bathrobe before taking my underwear off to get into my pajamas. Although he didn't say anything, Pierre must have found that process a little unusual. He probably thought I was shy, which would have been understating the obvious.

When we turned off the lights, I was ready for sleep but lay there for several minutes thinking about what a day it had been, leaving Mom and Dad, the trip, meeting students from all over the world and now, this good looking guy lying on top of his sheets in his underwear.

Early the next morning I opened my eyes to see Pierre wrapping a towel around his naked body as he headed for the showers. There was no way I was going to the showers like that. After he left the room I donned my bathrobe once again and was relieved when I opened the door to the hallway and saw other guys in bathrobes — carrying their towels instead of wearing them. I was more than a little relieved to arrive at the showers to find they consisted of rows of one-person stalls with doors.

I returned to my room shortly after Pierre and found him still drying himself with his towel. With my bathrobe still on, I slipped into my underwear and tried not to watch him. I certainly wanted to but was deathly afraid of him noticing me noticing him.

The seminary, consisting of several buildings, was surrounded by a thick forest of spruce and maple trees cut with miles of winding trails. My first experience entering those woods was both enchanting and emotional. My home town was a beautiful city with its streets lined with oak and maple trees and parks with willows and spruce, but here the trees intermingled to form a tapestry of colours, shapes and sizes. Each step was an invitation to take another, and another, walking farther and farther into the calm, constantly comforted by the forest floor of ferns, small flowers and mushrooms.

Marshes scattered throughout the woods were filled with the sounds of frogs and birds. This world was alive, not only with all of its many creatures, including white-tailed deer, but also with something else, something even more enchanting, more mysterious than the forest itself. I couldn't name it at the time but it left me overwhelmed with a sense of peacefulness. I felt no fear of any potential version of "the big bad wolf", or of getting lost because I was not alone — I was in a sacred place with God.

All of nature encircled and comforted me. I felt protected and safe to say or feel any emotion that came to the surface. Walking out of the woods made me feel like I was leaving someone behind, yet I knew He would be there when I returned.

Though the inside of a church had always been a very reverent place for me, it had never offered the same feeling of closeness to God that the woods did. In nature, I could look within myself and feel a relationship, a presence that offered me inner prayer and dialogue, and time alone with my God.

On our first Friday evening a conference was held with Father Louis-Marie Parent, the founder of the institute, presenting. I had met him briefly during the registration process. He spoke to us about spirituality and the spiritual framework of his institute, which he referred to as the 5-5-5. He had a sincere and kind presence about him and spoke passionately. He said 5-5-5 was an attitude to life and how we should view ourselves, our relationships with others, and with God. It was a powerful concept that I immediately took to heart.

Father Parent explained that the first "five" has to do with our relationship with God: our intimacy with the Lord through daily prayer, centred on the spiritual exercises of mental prayer or meditation; reading the word of God (the scriptures); the Eucharist (mass); devotion to the blessed sacrament (hour adorations); and devotion to the Virgin Mary, especially through fervent meditation on the mysteries of the rosary.

The second five, he explained, is an inner attitude or spirit of contemplation, of humility and fraternal charity expressed and nurtured through an awareness of the presence of God, an absence of criticism, absence of complaint, being of service, and being peacemakers.

The third five concerns our relationships with others. We are called to seize the opportunity every day to perform at least five concrete acts of charity in order to practise living our contacts with others in a positive manner, as Jesus taught us. We were not to be telling others that we were doing acts of charity for them; all that mattered was that we be aware that we were doing five acts of charity and of practising 5-5-5 every day.

A similar evening conference about "teams" was held on Saturday evening. We would be divided into groups of five or six, along with a third-year student as a team leader. Teams would meet weekly and members were supposed to support each other. At our first team meeting we would be assigned a "chore" for the month, then another at the beginning of every month thereafter in a rotational cycle.

Other topics of weekly team meetings turned out to be how we were managing with our studies, spiritual exercises, and subjects that we either wanted raised ourselves, or that the team leader or staff wanted us to discuss. And once a month, to keep up the team spirit, we'd go to a movie, out for a hike or to a restaurant, or challenge another team into a sporting activity.

When my team met for the first time, I thought we looked like the United Nations. I was Canadian, our group leader was from Sri Lanka, and the others were from France, Trinidad, Haiti and Laos.

At 9:45 the bells rang on the first Sunday morning. Cars were arriving with families that had come for Sunday mass, and with 60 students and 40 Oblate Sisters, we filled the church. It seemed like only a half hour later it was over, but more than an hour had passed. The solemnity of several priests celebrating together, with several seminarians as servers, and the contagious enthusiasm and the power of the singing almost brought me to tears. I was saddened to see it end.

In contrast, in my home parish our family had always attended the 9 a.m. mass, which consisted of the parish priest, who had probably just gotten out of bed, two altar servers, myself having been one of them, and the organist, who was accompanied by someone trying to lead a reluctant and unenthusiastic congregation in *How Great Thou Art* — a congregation that kept an eye on their watches, knowing it would be over soon and they could leave the church as enthusiastically as they had entered it.

But at the seminary, once that first mass was over, people mingled and welcomed back the students they had met the previous year, while also getting to know us new arrivals. As they left, they waved and shouted out to us in French, "A la semaine prochaine!" (See you next week!)

The experience was overpowering for me. Every day included attending a well-prepared celebration of mass, setting aside time to say the rosary, for meditation, private prayer, scriptural and spiritual reading; and all this interwoven in a day of study and community activities. The environment nourished me in a very rich, spiritual life.

Sunday evening we had the last "newcomers' conference, which was quite timely for me. The topic was "particular friendships". To that point in my life, I don't think I had ever thought of any of my friends as "particular friends". The message was that we were not to be friends with any one particular person, which meant not hanging around with the same person all the time for fear that others might feel excluded. Al, an American and someone I quickly befriended, looked over at me and smiled.

At the time, I was too naive to realize there was a lot more involved in the institute's concern about "friendliness" among the students; it was very closely related to my own concern about being attracted to males.

Not having any particular friends could not possibly make my life any more complicated than it already was so I didn't worry about it. Al and I did study together on a regular basis. That was partly because even though we both had French backgrounds, neither of us commonly spoke French, nor had we ever studied in French.

The French culture was in my blood and I understood my parents when they spoke French, but growing up in an English community in Ontario, I had spoken English at every opportunity. Al, an Acadian, had been raised in Boston and had had a similar experience.

We found ourselves being taught in French but English was our first language and we were both used to and more comfortable with English.

Life at the seminary was full of fraternal teasing and joking around. Everyone, at some point, became the subject of someone else's prank. Despite my childhood having lacked affection and affirmation, the one gift that my parents, especially Mom, gave to all of us was a sense of humour. My brother and sisters and I still have this innate ability to see humour almost anywhere, and to laugh at almost anything. That ability was as much a Godsend at the seminary as it had been at home.

One weekend, which had been designated as an "outing" for everyone to go and visit Quebec City or

Montreal, a few of us who had a natural connection to each other through all being rather loud, flamboyant and always laughing, decided to do something on our own. Our plan was to steal (no other way of saying it) a gallon of sacramental wine from the kitchen cooler and sneak down behind the seminary to a cabin that was used for small team meetings and as retreat space. Since no one was on retreat that weekend, we used the cabin as our outing destination.

But the plan had two flaws... actually three! First, none of us had ever drank a full glass of sacramental wine before, which has a high alcohol content.

Secondly, though we had gotten through a glass each without feeling any pain (Actually we were in pretty good spirits), we hadn't anticipated what it would be like after four or five glasses.

I, in particular, had a very low tolerance for sacramental wine — and a complete loss of mobility after four glasses.

By late evening when we decided it was time to return to the fold — the supply of wine having been depleted — we agreed that the one among us who could still walk on his own would be the forward lookout, moving strategically ahead, securing the way for the two who were helping me to navigate, and to keep quiet in the process. Thus, we continued back to the seminary, up the stairs and down the corridors to our rooms. If we met anyone, the plan was to say that we had had a good evening out, which was, we convinced ourselves, only a partial and small lie. Luckily, no one else was about at that hour.

Spending most of the rest of the night "hollering" into the porcelain telephone gave me painful pause enough to become aware of the third flaw of the adventure, and major lesson of the evening, which had to do with just how sick someone could get on sacramental wine.

By the following morning, word had gotten out, thanks to my colleagues in crime, that I was very ill. Our team leader, surprisingly not too concerned about the over imbibing, felt compelled to remind me of the dangers of particular friendships. Meanwhile, he, being from Sri Lanka, had frequently enjoyed being with other students from that part of the world. The rest of us had accepted that as natural, yet he saw our little group as a clique. His apparent jealousy bothered me because, in fact, each of us had been going out of our way to be friendly with everyone. But at the same time, I must admit, the sense of fraternity I felt with others in our little group was more than community; it felt more like family.

Shortly after arriving at the seminary, we had each been asked to choose a spiritual director from among the priests, someone who would be our personal mentor and confessor, with whom we would meet monthly, or more often if needed. I chose an elderly priest who was a professional graphologist and had long ago studied this science intently for three years before beginning counselling others based on an analysis of their handwriting. He and his art fascinated me.

With hindsight, he had been the perfect choice for me. He was a kind, forgiving and patient father image. He helped me understand what was being asked of me through the spirituality of the institute. He knew through analysis of my handwriting what I wasn't saying, yet he just listened, encouraged and respected my silence and my secret.

I remember telling him of my surprise at everyone at the seminary hugging each other when we returned from holidays and how, at home, I had never been hugged like that, not even by my mother.

After speaking to him about my attraction to and love of the woods, he explained, "Ray, as an introvert, nature and the woods will always rejuvenate you because it is in them that you feel God's presence accepting you as you are."

I immediately thought of my secret and felt that he too, was probably aware of it. Along with God's presence in the woods, this man was part of my process of self-evaluation because he understood where I was coming from and was able to listen and counsel without judgment.

International students had never seen Canada's famous white stuff before. The branches of the spruce trees that first winter bent with the weight of their new covering of snow. The busy winter months passed quickly and even before the first signs of spring, seminarians from Quebec got quite excited at the prospect of preparing the maple trees and looking forward to maple-syrup time.

Being French, I identified with their excitement as I recalled how many years before, Mom had introduced us to this sweat delicacy. She used to get several cans of maple syrup from the area in Quebec where she had grown up. While she had been born in Maine, she had moved with her family to Quebec as a child. From her, I knew what the final product was like but had no idea about the process that produced it.

We soon found out what the old wooden shack in the woods was used for. Inside was a massive drum in the middle of the room, and a vent in the ceiling. We needed to tap the trees to collect the sap — forty gallons of sap to make one gallon of syrup. But you couldn't walk off the ploughed trails without snowshoes, which most of us had never used before, and even with them on, we sank down several inches. So, not only did we have to drill holes in each tree and place a tap and bucket for the sap to drip into, but we had to do it wearing snowshoes.

I loved the fraternity and camaraderie of the whole process. Everyone's laughing at each other for either not drilling deep enough into a tree, drilling on the wrong side, or falling and finding it difficult to get back up while in snowshoes all made the labour less like work and more like play.

Once started, the process required a lot of attention so the next few months were very busy. Many of us used our recreation time to maintain the wood supply needed for the fire under the drum, which we kept filling with sap. On sunny days, the warmth of the sun would cause the sap to drip more quickly so the trees needed more attention.

When the maple syrup was ready, it was poured through a funnel at the base of the drum into several bottles, which were for the kitchen staff, but some was poured in long thin strips onto a large pan filled with about two inches of patted snow in it. Then a popsicle stick was placed at the start of the strip and rolled, making a thick taffy popsicle; and what a treat it was!

We also broke eggs into boiling syrup and then scooped them up and poured syrup over pancakes and desserts. It was a most anticipated time of the year and quite a treat for all of us, especially for those from other countries.

Just before my second summer at the seminary, my parish priest arranged with the Religious Sister at the Catholic hospital in my home town for me to work there as an orderly for the summer. Getting VIP treatment and skipping the normal employment channels of working for a few weeks or a month at a time at different vineyards and fruit orchards in southern Ontario, depending on the needs of the farmers, left me very grateful, and my mother was ecstatic to have me nearby!

I enjoyed the job, though giving a sponge bath to a young, well-endowed man proved a bit awkward. He got an erection while I was washing his genital area. He sheepishly apologized as his face reddened considerably.

"It happens," was all I could say, but I was thinking, *"Thank you, I'm flattered."*

Though he was definitely more uncomfortable than me, it was the first time I had ever been in the presence of a man with a hard-on. I wondered why it had happened to him in particular and quickly realized the whole incident would have to remain our secret.

Being an orderly offered me the opportunity to experience myself as a compassionate person. Many of the patients just wanted someone to speak to and listen to their concerns. I was uncomfortable not knowing what to say to them but always managed a smile and to wish them well before moving on to my next task. I felt comfortable in that environment and was soon sent to different parts of the hospital to help out.

One day, the administrator asked me if I would be willing to work with Dr. Brown?

"What department is he in?" I asked.

"The morgue," she replied, and without a second thought, I accepted and was soon talking to Dr. Brown.

"Ray," he asked right off the bat, "have you ever seen a deceased person before?"

"At a distance," I answered.

"So why did you accept this job?"

"I thought it would be a great opportunity to see the makeup of the human body first hand... and to understand why and how autopsies are done."

He raised an eyebrow as he looked at me, but just said he needed someone to assist him for the next few weeks because his regular assistant was on a leave of absence.

"When do I start," I asked with enthusiasm.

"Now," he said as he proceeded to give me a very quick tour of his department before handing me an apron.

"Put the cap and gloves on as well," he added as he walked toward a covered body on a steel table in the middle of the room. Then, with one hand holding the edge of the white sheet covering the body, he paused and asked, "Are you ready?"

"What will happen if I faint?"

"I'll leave you there until I'm finished."

"I'm ready," I said, and with that he removed the sheet, revealing a man's naked body. I expected an odor but it was minimized, I learned later, by keeping the room quite cool.

Dr. Brown then handed me the end of a rubber hose that led into a very large glass container and asked me to follow the scalpel with the open end of the hose, which would suction up any liquid as he began an incision.

The experience was almost unreal. Rather than wanting to faint, I was mesmerized as he opened the ribcage wide, exposing all the organs. I was in absolute awe, fixated on the organs, the colours, how compact and neatly fitted everything was.

At each step in verifying the cause of death, Dr. Brown explained what he was looking for. If an organ was discoloured, for example, that would lead to his looking for something else. Then we took the organs and weighed them, including the brain. I was amazed at the myriad of details involved. Then he sewed the body back up.

Throughout the whole process, Dr. Brown was as respectful of the individual he was working on as any loved one of the deceased might ever hope that he would be.

When I got home that day and told my parents about my promotion to the morgue, Mom said, "You call that a promotion," and we all had a good laugh.

The hospital experience made me feel alive, a part of something and less lonely, and the activity and variety of tasks excited and invigorated me.

2
Interludes

A Bite of the Big Apple

*M*y studies during the first three years at minor seminary focused on philosophy and a wide range of thinkers from Aquinas to Voltaire. We studied the Scriptures line by line. As future priests, we needed a thorough grounding in the Fathers of the Church, from Alexander the Great to Vincent of Lerins.

Then there were the studies of the seven sacraments, the seven deadly sins, the Ten Commandments, the doctrines and regulations that came from Vatican Councils; added to all that were the studies of moral ethics, Latin, the study of Jesus (Christology), of Mary (Mariology), of church history (ecclesiology), and basic psychology.

I was completely immersed in these studies, on a kind of autopilot. Christmas, Easter and the summer holidays came and went; the end of this phase of my life was fast approaching. All I needed to do was to continue studying, doing the 5-5-5, continue being accepted and, before realizing it, the priesthood and all that that would involve would be upon me. And with that thought, I felt more and more like a part of me was being cut away, sacrificed, that a part of me didn't belong. The old feeling of being alone resurfaced.

On each visit home, my parents met me at the terminal where my habitual hug for Mom was habitually not reciprocated, and I simply shook Dad's hand. Initially, we would all be happy and excited about seeing each other again and the first evening would be spent catching up with news about the family, distant relatives, and the neighbours. However, my mother was soon at me with relentless persistence.

"Ray, call these people, they have been asking about you and they would really like to see you."

In hindsight, I believe my reluctance to fall into the role she expected of me came from my soul's yearning to be fully and honestly myself, to shed the secret and damn the consequences. I didn't completely understand that at the time so it's no wonder she didn't. Mom just returned my reticence with a look of disappointment and further insistence. It was always about her at any rate.

"Every time I see them they ask about you and say they are praying for you," she would say. "If they knew you were home and didn't call them, what would I say to them?"

She would look at me in her own certain way and trigger the same emotions I had had before ever leaving for the seminary. My reluctance to visit everyone on her list increased with each return visit and she would confront me every time.

"Ray," I don't know why you bother coming home, every time you come back, you're worse."

What she wanted was for me to reflect well on her, to make a "good impression" in the community as a seminarian, which would always leave me standing there in disbelief and hurt.

As for Dad, in his loyalty and devotion to the church, he would have made a great crusader, not that I would have been proud of him for it. My studies included church history, the popes and the crusades, which I tried to share with him, but he always insisted, "The church must have been right in what it did because the Pope was doing the Will of God."

Even relationships with my old friends changed. They wanted to hear about my studies but couldn't understand how I could choose a life without women — and I was unable to tell them I simply couldn't see myself having a life with a woman.

My first Christmas visit home did have its positive side. The priests were expecting me at the church for weekday morning mass at 8:30 a.m. the day after my arrival. After mass, they invited me to serve at the upcoming Christmas midnight mass and the three masses on Christmas Day so they could introduce me to parishioners. When I returned home with this news, Mom was beside herself with glee.

I was struck with disbelief myself at being handed the Christmas Midnight Mass and the three Masses on Christmas Day!

Most of the time, however, I was torn between the excitement of wanting to be home to share my experiences, and the conflicts I seemed to create by being there. With each visit, Mom seemed to find me more independent and opinionated, which she didn't much like. I was fighting to become my own person but her expectations of me as a seminarian dominated my time at home. Invariably, I fought back tears on the bus ride back to the seminary.

With all my internal conflict after completing minor seminary, I was not eager to immediately continue with the remaining four years of studies in theology. Instead, those old thoughts of pursuing monasticism kept coming to the surface. To try to find some clarity, I discussed the options with my spiritual director, who listened attentively. I told him the prospect of continuing my studies right then made me feel caught, very alone, and scared.

"And I don't really know why," I said.

"Ray, follow your heart," he responded compassionately, "and be open, that God may call you back here, and I will support your decision."

With that said, plans were made for me to spend the summer at Our Lady of the Genesee Monastery in Geneseo, New York, and experience the Trappist community during the summer before returning to the major seminary — if God didn't call me to be a monk in the meantime.

I flew home to meet my family, who then drove me to Rochester, New York, and on to Geneseo, which rambles through rolling valleys that stretch as far as the eye can see. The landscape is patched with cattle ranges and thick forested areas that give shade to the livestock. It was a beautiful, though very long drive on that day in 1967; we were beginning to fear we were on the wrong road when suddenly, there it was, the monastery stood about a half mile off the main road.

We were met by a monk who asked us to go to the residence on the other side of the road, which was a beautiful building that dated back to the American Civil War era — a plantation in its own right — surrounded by massive weeping willows. We had arrived at the guesthouse.

A few monks shared their time with us, showing my family and I the property, my guest room, and the monastery gift shop, which sold "Monks' Bread", their main source of income. My parents' purchases of it, along with other items made by the monks, especially cheese and chocolates, generously supported the enterprise.

When it was time to say goodbye to my family, the look of disbelief in my brother's eyes that I was actually going to stay in this place was unmistakable.

"It's so quiet," he kept saying.

My mother, though she seemed to appreciate the silence, shared his sense of disbelief at what I was embarking upon.

That evening after their departure, the soft breeze and the warmth of the day were the perfect incentive for a stroll down by a large fish pond situated beyond the guesthouse among some magnificent, huge willows. My sense of peace and connection was immediate but I wasn't there long when the silence was broken by a strong male voice.

"May I join you?" he asked. My name is Henri Nouwen... and yours?"

"I'm Ray... Buteau," I replied hesitatingly.

Henri Nouwen was a writer visiting the monastery for the first time, apparently to work on a manuscript. At the time, I think I must have been the only seminarian who didn't know who he was. While we were there together, he offered me the opportunity to read excerpts from his manuscript. *Cry for Mercy.*

Henri took an interest in who I was, in my background and my studies. We enjoyed the evening under the willows, and did so on many subsequent, wonderful occasions, having lengthy talks on spirituality or just chatting casually as friends. He returned in 1971 and stayed for seven months while he wrote the *Genesee Diary.* But while our paths and life experiences crossed again over the years, we never meet again.

Thirty-one years later, I studied the writings, especially his book *Wounded Healer,* and learned again the importance of just "being present" to others.

And forty years later, I discovered that Henri and I had been living the same spiritual struggle and pain of being "alone" in not having been able, as priests, to live out our lives with a significant other. I eventually learned that we also shared the same secret, and that we were not the only two priests with that secret.

My first day at the monastery was as surreal as my first day had been at the seminary years before. Even though the monks were not to have idle chatter among themselves, I picked up on a strong sense of fraternity among them and quickly learned that charity toward monks within a monastery is to respect their need for silence.

They gathered in the chapel seven times a day for prayer — The Divine Office (liturgy of the hours) was recited in Gregorian Latin chant. The lights were always dimmed when they entered the church and made their profound bow of adoration to the altar and cross, then moved silently to their stalls to pray, sitting, kneeling, or squatting on their heels in their large, tan-coloured garments with the big hoods, which dated back to the twelfth century.

The atmosphere of silence and prayerfulness within the natural setting of the monastery, encircled as it was by rolling hills and miles of trails through beautiful forests comforted me a great deal. Wallowing in the profound spiritual experience, I found myself loosing track of time.

The Voluntas Dei Institute had its 5-5-5 and the monks had their 8-8-8: eight hours of prayer, eight hours of work, and eight hours of sleep. They considered their work to be part of their recreation in that work offered a lot of exercise.

One day they put me on a tractor to plough a small field. All went well until I tried to stop and couldn't, so I kept ploughing along the road, heading straight for the monastery! Finally, a monk spotted me and came running to my rescue; fortunately for both of us, I had been ploughing very slowly.

My second job was in the bakery. My task was to take the loaves of bread off a conveyor belt and put them in stacking trays. Again, all went well until the bread got ahead of me and started to backlog. Desperate to halt the growing mountain of manna, I hit a red stop button on the wall, not realizing that it stopped everything, including all the ovens full of baking bread that had been kept slowly rotating so as not to burn.

So then they tried me in the cattle stalls, pitchfork in hand. A month of relative success there found me promoted back to the bakery — but with a monk between me and the red button.

While working or during other regular activities, interactions at the monastery were never distracted by idle chatter or indiscrete questions or comments; we just accepted each other's presence. The simplicity of the lifestyle struck me — no one had unnecessary possessions or nicnacs, which kept their living spaces, and their minds, uncluttered. Like the woods, they too, accepted my presence in silence.

I was well accepted by the community of monks and there was an interest in my returning, but I hadn't realized at the time that there was a minimum age requirement of 25 years, and I was just 23. The monks suggested that in the interim, I could apply for a position with a Catholic organization (The Techo Foundation), a branch of the American Peace Corps that would require a two-year commitment from me.

They suggested that two years and more experience of life would help me decide if I really wanted to enter their order when I turned 25.

While still at the monastery, all the arrangements were made for me to enter The Techo Foundation (Spanish for roof/shelter). My parents were surprised that I would be accepted based only on my mother's American citizenship, and even more surprised at my willingness to go ahead with the plan rather than return to my studies.

The contact priest for the Techo Foundation met me in Manhattan and drove me to Briarcliff Manor in Ossining, N.Y., a very exclusive part of the upper city. He said the mansion I would be staying at had been part of the Rockefeller Estate. We drove up to a high stone fence with a large, decorative, black metal gate that opened to a driveway that circled in front of the three-storey, medieval-looking castle. With a smile, he said, "Welcome to your new home, Ray."

"And what a magnificent home it must have been," I thought as we entered the lobby, with its regal spiral staircase before me. My companion priest wished me well on our way to one of the offices to fill out forms and to sign a two-year contract, which required taking an oath of secrecy stating that any "pertinent information" whatever that might be, would be given directly to the director and to no one else.

We were fifteen young adults studying Spanish and the culture of Chile, which was where we were to be sent. Men were on a separate floor from the women and each floor was off limits to the other. My room met my needs: a comfortable bed, a desk, a recliner, and a large window overlooking a forested area, which comforted me as I settled in.

We met in the lounge for an orientation and to be given a tour of the mansion. It included a classroom, a lounge area, a library, dining area and a massive ballroom that was used for charity events that we would be hosting to support our project in Chile. While sitting in the lounge, we were given the opportunity to introduce ourselves and to tell the others how we had found out about Techo... and to hear about how this sole Canadian had gotten in. What we had most in common was our idealism, good intentions, and a keen interest in volunteering our services in another country.

We were given a study timetable, books and tapes to study Spanish, and reference material on Chile. Our church services were at one of two nearby institutions: Kings College, which has since burned down and been relocated, and the Maryknoll Missionary Centre for priests preparing for work in Asian countries.

After only two weeks into the program, because of the political situation in Chile, our project there was suspended. Instability in the country eventually led to a bloody coup in September, 1973, ending Chile's democratic government and installing the ruthless dictator Augusto Pinochet.

As our new project, we would be divided into two groups and work in small secondhand clothing stores in the Bronx to gather information about tenement housing in the area and report our findings back to the director.

Working at the store was nothing like I had ever before experienced. I had never met gypsies for one thing, and knew nothing about their European origins or cultural characteristics. They looked a lot like street people to me, and they had what I thought was a Slavic accent. I was told they were great at bartering and loved to argue pricing so I was warned that it was important not to get upset, and to gain their respect by at least trying to barter with them.

I spotted my first gypsy by her attire as she piled up three boxes full of clothing. Having been forewarned, I wondered what to charge for each article. She had other intentions. Sizing up this naive 23-year-old, she called me over.

"I give you good business," she began. "I pay for two boxes and you give me one box free."

I paused to do my own sizing up, then replied, "I'll make you a deal... you pay for these two boxes, and if you don't want to pay for this other box, you can leave it here until you can pay for it."

With that, she launched into a raging verbal attack, ending with, "I'll tell my friends that you're not a good person!" She left the three boxes, and me, looking bewildered. One of the other workers came up to me smiling.

"You'll see her here tomorrow," he warned, and sure enough, she was back the next day. At first I was a bit apprehensive, fearing a conflict but she merely stepped up and paid for all three boxes.

When we weren't working we were given money and day passes to downtown New York City. Yes, the Big Apple! I was young, adventurous, and very naïve. After doing the sightseeing tours and walking in Time Square, I caught sight of all the magazines being sold from a small street-corner newsstand. I soon spotted one with three young men in bathing suits standing very close together.

"May I see that magazine?" I asked nervously.

"Are you over eighteen?" the attendant asked.

"Yes," came my meek reply to the question, which seemed rather odd at the time.

As I opened the magazine, my heart started pounding as my eyes stared at men having sex with each other. Other pictures immediately conjured fantasies in my mind.

After what must have seemed like a lot of gasping on my part, he asked, "Are you going to buy it or hand it back?"

"I'll take it," I said sheepishly.

With a huge, knowing smile, he asked, "Would you like me to put it in a bag?"

"Yes... please," I said.

Throughout the magazine, I found the names of bookstores, bars, and bath houses... whatever *they* were!

On my next day pass, I headed straight for Greenwich Village, which was a world of its own, and walked into my first gay bar. I drank my beer nervously, playing with the coaster while trying to look around as nonchalantly as possible. I was among others like myself, I knew that, but I was too shy and emotional to speak to anyone. I listened intently, absorbing how they spoke and behaved. While my level of anxiety was high, it all felt good, like I belonged. In spite of my insecurity and apprehension with the situation, that place felt comfortable to me in a way that I struggled to understand.

Oddly, I was reminded of how, as a teen, we would ride our bikes from St. Catharines to Niagara Falls. Along the way we would stop by the orchards and help ourselves to some of the fruit from the trees along the road. The farmers wouldn't mind as long as we didn't take a basketful with us. There was no harm in picking a large, ripe red Mackintosh from a big apple tree and savouring that first, particularly juicy bite of forbidden fruit - something "off limits," yet strongly desired.

My next visit to the village in search of another bath house took me through neighbourhoods and down side streets that I was too naïve to know could have been dangerous. The address was right, but there was no sign indicating a name, only a red light above a door. I followed two men in and, once inside, found another door in front of us. To our left, a man sat at a counter behind a cage-like screen.

"Room or locker," he asked the two ahead of me. They asked for a room.

"And you?" he asked me, barely bothering to look up. "The same," I replied, not knowing any different. I paid and he handed me a key and towel and buzzed me into the lobby. "Could you tell me where to find this room? This is my first time here," I said.

A man standing nearby said he would show me the way. Favours don't come without a price, and they certainly didn't in that place.

The hallways were very dark. Once inside my room, I locked the door behind me. While taking off my clothes, I could hear moans and groans even through the loud background music.

There was a locker for all my belongings. With only a towel on and a key on a wrist band, I was ready to leave the room.

Other men starred at me, some smiling and others nodding their heads. Not knowing how to respond, I kept walking around, passing opened doors to rooms with men lying on beds, some with, and others without their towels on. I smiled, too naïve to know better.

Finally, I found a place to sit and watch how others behaved, trying to understand how they were communicating and acting. A very good looking man about ten years older than me introduced himself.

"This is my first time in a place like this," I said, admitting the obvious with an appropriate nervous quiver in my voice. He probably thought, *Lucky me!* "Would you like me to show you the place?" he asked.

Again too naïve to know better, I gave him the reply he was looking for. "Yes, I would," I said.

He showed me all the back rooms and explained the subtle language of eye and body language. He seemed to want to befriend me and spend time talking. He offered me a drink and we went to the lounge to sit and watch the porn video that was playing. Sitting close to him and watching porn was quite arousing for both of us. He had years of experience over me and had his own intentions in taking me under his wing. I learned a great deal that day, including some valuable lessons about the games people play to get what they want. He got what he wanted and, after the apple was bitten, I was no longer a virgin.

It wasn't the way I had imagined it would be in my fantasies with Steve McQueen. Caught up in the erotic sexual high energy of the place, I hadn't been prepared for the kind of intense encounter in which I felt I was about to pass out.

Afterwards, my partner seemed kind and caring toward me, wanting to buy me another drink and continue chatting to get to know me better. But my only thought was to escape from what had become my new reality, and from the new awareness of how naïve and alone I was. Not only had there never been anyone with whom to share my secret, but there was also no one I could talk to about my first sexual encounter.

I fretted over how I was ever to meet others like me in Canada? Were there even any magazines like the one I had found in New York? For the moment, I took solace in knowing that in the broader world at least, I was not alone, and could enjoy New York while I was there.

Working in the secondhand clothing store was generally pretty quiet, aside from having to be on your toes with the gypsies, until the day three burly black cops came charging in to tell us to lock up and drive as quickly as possible out of the Bronx. As "whites" our lives were in particularly perilous danger in that black neighbourhood on that particular day.

"If anyone tries to stop your car just keep driving," one of them said.

"But why, what's going on?" someone asked.

"Do as you're told; you could be killed if you stay here!" came the loud response from an impatient officer.

We got the message and within seconds everyone's adrenaline was at full throttle as we ran for the car and went speeding through the neighbourhood trying to get to the highway as quickly as possible.

In that black community, pedestrians who caught sight of us waved their fists at us but we drove too quickly to react, speeding through stop signs and red lights as safely as we could.

Once on the throughway, someone finally had the presence of mind to turn on the radio.

Martin Luther King Junior had just been assassinated!

Back within the safety of the centre, my heart was still pounding, as I'm sure everyone's was, until we were given a debriefing session by the staff.

It was April 4 — my mother's birthday — so I called home.

"Happy Birthday Mom," I said as soon as she picked up the phone, then quickly moved on. "Have you heard about what just happened?"

Like a large part of the world that day, Mom was in a state of disbelief. I told her about the excitement of my day and how it would not be safe to return to the store at all. As it turned out, that store was destroyed by angry neighbours and we had to be assigned to another project. We had a few days to process the reality of what we had been a part of — though far from the site of the actual assassination, we had been among the people for whom Martin Luther King Jr. had had a dream.

The personal experiences in The Big Apple had helped to connect me to that part of myself I had felt I had been "cutting away" at minor seminary. That was good, but I had problems with the organization. I had signed up for a project in Chile, not two years in the Bronx under an oath of secrecy that I was not comfortable with at all. Now there would be another assignment to another used clothing store and more secrecy. I had had enough and, despite the director reminding me that I had signed a two-year contract and to leave at that point would mean I would not be allowed to apply for another project with any American agency, I quit. I had had enough!

It was 1968 and I was only 24 years old. I couldn't return to the monastery, and I was cutting my ties with The Techo Foundation so, to Mom's relief, I decided to continue my studies and enter major seminary back home.

Major Seminary

The decision to return to my studies, and getting back into the spirituality of the institute felt right, though I was certainly not as innocent as I had been when I left. Knowing there were others like me "out there" also felt good.

A seminarian met me in Perth Andover, New Brunswick, to drive me to the Institute Voluntas Dei major seminary in Red Rapids, N.B. As we drove, we were encircled by rolling hills, narrow roads with rock cliffs bordering them, and forests that seemed endless. Periodically, a farmyard appeared next to large fields of red soil.

After travelling half an hour through the rolling countryside, to my right, at the top of a high hill, the two-storey, long brick buildings that formed the major seminary campus came into view. As we took my luggage to my room, I began meeting friends who were now a year ahead of me after my "sabbatical" in New York. Classes would begin in a few days so I had time to settle in and re-orientate myself. The priests were young, and one in particular was very good looking.

As in minor seminary, most of the seminarians were international students. The mix of nations in our team, the cleaning chores, visits to the merchants for food supplies, the 5-5-5, the team meetings, the fraternity, the evaluations, were all familiar to me. But there were differences. We were told, for example, that first-year students would form a parish team and assist a priest from the seminary in serving several families in the immediate area who attended our Sunday services. The other seminarians were also divided into parish teams with priests from the seminary, assisting the parishes and missions in the diocese in more general ways.

We would be giving children and adults religious instruction, preparing them for the Sacraments of Initiation (first communion, first confession and confirmation) and to be altar servers. The teens formed a youth group with their own activities and socials. And along with leading the congregation in singing, we would greet everyone as they entered and left the church. We would also have opportunities to visit families and shut-ins.

As it unfolded, team meetings were often attended by the priest who was part of our parish team and our spiritual director. The meetings gave each of us the opportunity to share our reactions and concerns about the experiences we were having, not only at the seminary, but also in the parish setting. We experienced the positive aspects of parish ministry, including the respect and gratitude of the people. Unfortunately, it was a false indication of how we would often be treated as parish priests in later years because we were not exposed to the administration and politics within a parish community and a diocese. I was naïve to think that entering major seminary would really give me a better idea of what the priesthood would be all about.

Our studies in scripture, sacramental preparation, dogma and ethics were more intense than they had been in minor seminary. Besides our practical pastoral experience, we were given courses in public speaking, homiletics, and catechetical teaching. There was a sense of serious preparation for ordination in just a few years.

The studies about God and the Roman Catholic Church had often seemed to me like a process of dissecting an animal and studying every organ. I would regularly ask myself if a relationship with God was really that complicated. This was not a hospital morgue, after all. Would the process lead me to feeling any closer to God; closer than I felt just soaking up the natural beauty of the area, with its panoramic sea of colour in the fall, the red soil of the fields in spring; the congested growth of green potatoes plants ready for harvest by late summer?

For me, God was easily accessible in the breathtaking autumn scenery with the maple trees revealing the best of their reds, oranges, yellows and browns as far as the eye could see in any direction. By mid fall the walking trails were rivers of crackling, ankle deep leaves still sporting their splendid colours. Being a part of it all was, indeed, a spiritual experience.

In winter, the spruce trees were weighed down with a thick covering of fluffy, powdery, sparkling snow. The paths were kept clear for walking and in the evening when the moon reflected off the snow, you could clearly see into the depth of woods and the small river running through them. Being a part of it all was, indeed, a spiritual experience.

In contrast, during our studies, frequent reference was made to us as being "another Christ", to being the representatives of Jesus on earth, leaders and models of church authority. We were "in the world but not of the world." That notion made me feel somewhat separated from the parishioners, being made to believe that I was somehow closer to God as his servant and representative on earth than they were. In nature, I felt his presence in a way that comforted me much more than the theological ideals and catchy slogans.

Before entering my fourth year at major seminary, my soul nagged me constantly: *"Are you ready to deal with adults and their life issues and concerns, let alone a generation of young people searching for truth and independence?"*

My mind would not rest: *"And your secret, how are you going to deal with it 'in the world but not of the world'? You're different from those around you, Ray."*

My soul was anxious about my not being "of the world" if that meant somehow "leaving" the world that had others in it like me, though I was not connected with any of them at the time. I spoke with my spiritual director about the possibility of gaining more clarity about my future through more pastoral experience before resuming the formal, academic journey toward ordination. I suspect I was having last minute cold feet about becoming an ordained priest and taking my secret into that world, but he supported the idea and I was off to Manitoba.

I was granted permission to stay at the bishop's residence in St. Boniface until I could find my own lodgings. My hosts had already been informed of my having successfully completed my third year of theology, of not having been attached to any diocese, and looking for pastoral experience. They greeted me as a potential candidate, especially since I was bilingual in French-speaking St. Boniface.

Soon after finding work with the local Age and Opportunity as an outreach worker at a Senior Citizens' Centre, the Bishop asked, "Ray, would you be willing to do weekend pastoral work in one of our parishes?"

I said yes and thanked him.

"You'll be assigned to Blessed Sacrament Parish, a facility that serves two parishes, one Catholic and the other Anglican," he said.

It was my first experience with this kind of ecumenism and gave me the opportunity to meet many families from both communities, some of whom remained friends for many years.

The folks at the seniors' centre were mostly of Ukrainian and Polish background. They were a proud people with strong traditions and heritage. The elderly ladies treated me like a grandchild, spoiling me with baking and beautiful crafted gifts. They were also knowledgeable about life and insightful from years of experience. They reminded me of my dad because they often appreciated someone taking the time to listen to them. That was all part of the "up-side" of the experience.

However, also like Dad, many were also often biased and self-righteous. A discussion could often turn into a heated argument with anyone who thought differently, which was uncomfortable.

But then, once again like Dad, by the next day, all was forgotten.

It was during that time in Winnipeg that I was introduced to Omer at a gathering of Oblate missionary priests. I had occasionally expressed an interest in working with aboriginal people and Omer had heard about it..

"Ray," he asked me, "would you be willing to make a commitment to working for me for two and a half years up north?" "Where up north?" I responded.

"In a community called Repulse Bay."

"And that is where, exactly?"

"On the Arctic Circle," he said.

"With the Eskimos?"

"They refer to themselves as 'Inuit' nowadays," he replied. "And you work in the area as well?" I inquired.

With a smile and a surprised look at my question, he announced, "I'm the Bishop of the Arctic."

"When would I leave?"

"In three days."

"I'll be ready," I said.

Omer was pleased, but Mom? Not so much! When I called her with my news, all she could say was, "Oh no Ray! The Arctic?"

Not a Tree in Sight

❧

T hree days later, all I could see out the window of the plane for endless, mesmerizing miles was a terrain of white and grey with patches of blue. Finally, a break in the scenery came when I caught sight of a large herd of caribou running at full speed, as if being chased. The plane turned, descended sharply, and a village appeared along a shoreline. I could see no roads leading in or out of the community.

"This place is in the middle of nowhere," I thought.

As we touched down on a narrow gravel airstrip I could see several Mongolian-like faces with all sorts of expressions I didn't know how to interpret. Everyone was in parkas with fur-trimmed hoods of various colours. Mothers carried small children in large hooded attachments on their backs; all were anticipating the arrival of the plane and the Kabloonas — the "whites" from the south.

Stepping out of the plane on the Arctic Circle was an overwhelming experience. People greeted each other by touching noses or giving pats on the shoulder, uttering unusual sounds, laughing and teasing. When they looked toward me, some smiled, but without a word, and often with only a quick glance, as if I couldn't or shouldn't be acknowledged.

It was a dull and grey day. I was standing on grey rock surfaces with snow patches here and there. The snow was coarse, not powdery like I was used to down south. The gusting wind was very cold and lifted a veil of snow around the village just a short distance away. As a skidoo approached pulling a sled, the plane began taking off I was alone with the local priest, Father Rivoie, OMI, who had arrived on the skidoo to welcome me and begin his duties as my mentor. As he loaded my luggage onto the sled I wondered what I had got myself into.

"Ready or not, I am here," I thought as we drove into the community.

The first building I saw was a two-level home with aluminum siding and modern storm windows; it was the mission house. The "manager" of the community had a similar home, and there was one for a teacher and principal, and another for the nursing station. The Inuit homes were a mixture of four-room, box- like homes, some bungalows, others looking like small huts. They lined streets that looked like rolling hills of packed snow, some reaching the roof lines of the homes.

Many of the homes were painted various colours, but without fences or discernable boundaries between them, each property blended into the next. Skidoos, nets, animal carcasses, caribou antlers, and boards with hides stretched on them surrounded every house; many had animal carcasses on their roofs to keep stray dogs from getting at them. Long chains tethered to the ground had dogs tied along their lengths.

As we came into the village, skidoos roared about randomly, some on the rolling, snow-packed streets, some between the homes. There didn't seem to be any rules of the road. As well, large bombardiers pulling water supplies or collecting garbage moved up and down the street. Their most unusual cargo was what was known locally as "honey bags" — toilet waste left outside to freeze for easier collection.

And in the midst of all this activity were "the people", which is what the word "Inuit" means. With their round faces, tanned skin and high check bones, they looked like a proud people. A nod of the head or a raising of the eyebrows, a smile and a guttural "eee" sound indicated greeting as we passed them in the street. Younger women were quite beautiful, the men handsome and strong. Elders were weathered from lives spent in the elements. Children ran everywhere, teasing the dogs, each other, and before long, the new kabloona.

Not much of a conversationalist, Father Rivoie simply said "Supper is ready," as we disembarked from the skidoo to enter the mission. The rooms were simple and sparse, with basic furnishings; they were almost monastic, yet clean and comfortable. The only decorative touch was lots of plants. Father Rivoie was a botany buff.

We sat at the dinner table and said a prayer, then out came a large caldron filled with pigs' feet — my first of many "gourmet" meals. Father Rivoie had arrived from

France as a young man about thirty years before and such meals were a reminder of his homeland.

After several minutes with my pigs' feet, I ventured to break the silence.

"Father, I found it strange that no one said anything to me when I arrived; why was that?"

"They will watch and observe you," he replied.

"For how long?"

"Maybe a few days, weeks... as long as they want," he replied, remaining focused on his meal.

"This will give you time to settle in," he continued. "I started the co-op store for the carving and fur trade... you can help out over there while you learn the language and customs. The people know you have been sent here by the bishop and that you will be helping at the mission."

"I don't know how to greet or meet the people," I said with some concern.

"If people look at you, just smile and nod your head in recognition. The children won't hesitate to ask you questions. The women may feel uncomfortable acknowledging you because they won't know your intentions."

We continued for some time with my first lesson in cultural awareness and etiquette.

"When walking around the village or along the shoreline, if you see people unloading a sled or boat, start helping in whatever way you can, and afterwards, don't wait to be thanked. There are no Inuit words for please and thank you; what you will have done is expected. And don't wait to be invited or accepted, they need time to see how patient and persistent you are, just smile as you nod and leave.

"If you are invited in for tca, don't wait to be served, pour your own... it's a sign that you are accepting their hospitality."

Similar lessons went on day after day for weeks and weeks. I worked in the store, studied the language and culture, spent time with other "whites" in the community, walked around the village helping in small ways, went for walks, and explored the shoreline and local terrain.

"I believe in God, only I spell it 'nature"
— **Frank Lloyd Wright**

One day it struck me that there were no trees anywhere. I had been so caught up in the new world, with its different culture and people and new sights at every turn, so captivated by the absolute beauty and serenity of what seemed at first to be a barren world, I really hadn't noticed the absence of trees. Yet, I felt God's presence as profoundly as I had in the south with all of its forests and foliage. Then I also realized I had connected with the landscape, but felt distant from the people. I asked Father Rivoie when I would know that they had accepted me.

"I feel as if I'm just existing here, though it doesn't seem to bother anyone else," I said.

"Time is not an issue here," he calmly replied. "Take advantage of the time to observe and learn."

I was walking around the village a few months later when a man my age, twenty-eight at the time, invited me in for tea. The main room of his home served as a kitchen and living room. With my back to the living room area, I poured myself some Red Rose tea. I turned and headed for an empty chair that seemed to be waiting for me; it faced eight or nine men and women of various ages, all staring at me, some with their parkas still on, some with smiles of acceptance, others with looks of curiosity. But all eyes were fixed on me.

The room had been completely silent since I entered. No conversation was taking place. Unlike what any "southerner" might have expected, no introductions were made with small-talk comments about who everyone was and perhaps what they did for a living. I felt very out of place but, not knowing what to say or do, I just sat there smiling and drinking my tea.

Finally, without a word being said, I was offered a small piece of meat. Everyone's eyes were fixed on me as I accepted, popped it into my mouth and began chewing. My mouth quickly became filled with a liquid and when I passed a finger over my lips I was surprised to see blood on it, and immediately could also taste it. Another piece was offered, also in silence. Again, I didn't know what to say or do so I just sat and accepted, drawing on a great deal of faith that I would have the courage for whatever I was about to experience.

After I had eaten the meat and drank some more tea, we sat in silence for a few minutes, then the man next to me called the only child over to him. She was a lovely, frail-looking, shy child of about ten. As she approached him, with the back of his hand he struck her hard in the face, sending her flying to the floor. All eyes were on me; I felt numb and stunned.

The young girl placed her hand on her face and, without a whimper, went and sat on the floor in the corner of the room. No one consoled her. I couldn't believe what I was seeing; no emotion was shown by anyone, only the intensity of several eyes still fixed on me. I felt so helpless and confused. Why were they putting me through this?

A few minutes later I was led to the door by the one who had invited me in. As I began walking away, with a smile he said, "We are going hunting" and closed the door — no "goodbye", "see you tomorrow" or "come again", nothing that I could relate to. I left without understanding what had just happened, or if I would ever be invited back. I didn't like that encounter and was anxious to share the experience with Father Rivoie.

"That was frozen seal meat," he said when I asked about the meat I had been given. "It's filled with blood vessels and, as it thawed in your mouth, it expanded and you could taste the blood."

"Why was it given to me?"

"They wanted to see if you would eat whatever they gave you and how you would react."

When I described the shocking incident with the young girl, he said, "I'm sorry you were put through that. I've never heard of them doing that to another white person before."

"It seemed so cruel and I felt so helpless, I was afraid of saying or doing anything for fear of not being accepted."

"That is exactly why they did it," he said. "They wanted to see if you would judge their values according to yours, and how you would react."

"I was too stunned and scared to react at all... and why did they tell me they were going hunting?"

"What they were saying was that *you* are going hunting with them."

"When?"

"Any time... and you need to be ready."

Before going to bed that night I prepared my "caribou clothing," which had been given to me for extreme weather and any lengthy periods to be spent outdoors. It was traditional clothing worn by the Inuit while out hunting caribou. But I had no idea when they would arrive, I had trouble sleeping. It seemed I had only just dozed off when I was awakened by the sound of skidoos and barking dogs.

"Ray, get ready, they're here," Father Rivoie hollered from outside my room.

I headed outside quickly, wearing all my fur clothing: a parka, pants, footwear and mitts. Four or five skidoos were waiting, each pulling a sled loaded with provisions stacked two feet high and covered with furs tightly bound with rope to the sled runners. Everyone acknowledged Father Rivoie, showed me where to sit on one of the sleds, and with a sudden jolt and a quick wave, we were on our way.

It felt quite odd, unlike any trip I had ever taken. I was travelling with no luggage, not knowing where I was going, for how long, or what I was in for. In fact, I didn't really know with whom I was travelling. Yet I felt cared for and safe. I had only one thought: *"Ray, don't fall off"*

As the sled jostled in different directions, the men on either side of me showed me how to balance myself and how to keep my face to the side so as not to freeze it looking directly into the wind. There was no idle chatter, only teasing, poking, acting as if they were trying to knock me off the sled, and handing me pieces of meat to eat — no options were offered. I learned that it was all to keep me alert and warm; the teasing and eating were quite normal activity on such a trip.

After what seemed like hours, we stopped in the middle of nowhere, nothing in sight except the unbelievable beauty of the place. Suddenly I was in the midst of what seemed a bit like organized chaos. Some prepared boiling water for tea, others chased each other around, including me, some wrestled, others relieved themselves. Privacy was non-existent. This was an Arctic version of a highway "Husky" break, except this was not a gas station, and any huskies present had lots of fur and large teeth. After tea and a "pilot biscuit" we were off as quickly as we had stopped.

I had already learned not to take my watch with me in order to "see" the time. Time didn't seem to exist, it just was. The Inuit, while in the village, had noticed me constantly looking at the time. As days went by I would hear comments like, "Is it time for the Kabloona to eat?" (or work, sit down, go to the bathroom). When I mentioned these odd comments to Father Rivoie, he laughingly said they were teasing me for looking at my watch so often. To the Inuit, things were done because they needed to be done, not because it was time to do them.

After the "rest stop", having learned how to keep my balance under control, I was better able to appreciate the breathtaking view. As far as the eye could see, in all directions, an ethereal blue glow reflected the moon's light off the snow, reminding me of pictures of the moon's surface taken by astronauts. Then the northern lights began darting everywhere, over and around us in vivid colours of red, blue, yellow, green and white, like a shimmering sheet blowing in the wind. I felt I could almost touch them and even hear them as they swished through the crisp frigid air. It was a powerful spiritual experience.

It was late when we made another stop, this time alongside a few other skidoos and some dogs tied up close by. What at first seemed to be five-foot high mounds of snow were our rooms for the night — my first igloos. I crawled down a narrow shaft leading into a large round room. Once standing inside, I faced a higher level that was half the surface area of the room, like a waist-high, wall-to-wall table or bed. Lying in that area, with their heads all facing toward us in the "standing" area, were other men and women, half asleep, who acknowledged our arrival as they were told about me.

Following the lead of the others, I removed my outer parka and crawled under the furs with the rest of them on the raised level. I was in full culture shock, lying next to people I didn't even know, the heat of our bodies melding in between the furs, and all of us surrounded by a white dome. The absolute silence was broken only by the sounds of others sleeping and the occasional dog howling outside.

I was all too aware that I was next to very muscular, well- built and, I imagined, well-endowed men. Not knowing how they might react, I feared being caught in an embarrassing state of arousal. I was totally dependent on them for my survival and could not risk having my secret discovered. Because I was a seminarian, they had already accepted that I could not sleep with a woman. (Though offers were occasionally made, the thought repulsed me so it was easy to decline.)

Luckily, my exhaustion quickly became a sound sleep. In the morning, my friend, who had invited me on the hunting trip, asked me to follow him outside. He walked a short distance, squatted and relieved himself. He looked at me to do the same. With a smirk on his face, he threw me some moss, nature's substitute for toilet paper.

Privacy did not exist! Someone was around me at all times as I was taught, much like a child, how to survive in their world. Dutifully, I observed and imitated everything they did without question: how to clean myself, eat, prepare tea, load the sleds and, on this occasion, how to patch an igloo.

I was with a people who were very child-like but far from childish. They took delight in teasing, being spontaneous and carefree. If I was being tested by them it was so I could survive among them, not merely to achieve a passing or failing grade. To get annoyed or angry is a sign of weakness and rejection among the Inuit. Similarly, to accept the teasing and to be able to laugh at oneself are signs of strength and acceptance.

In the south, people often feel used by others, but in the Arctic, everyone is needed. In the south, people often tell others how much they love them, but in the Arctic, I could see that people were shown they were loved — words were not needed. It was wonderful not having to "perform" well to be accepted; I just had to "be".

I felt as if I was watching a movie, not knowing what the next scene would bring, but knowing I would be in it. Events happened quickly, unexpectedly, with no time between takes. Scene followed scene and I played my part, trying my best to follow the script. Whether digging through five feet of ice to fish, waiting motionless to spear a seal alongside a hole in the ice, laying traps for foxes and rabbits, or shooting ptarmigans, caribou, and polar bears, the days and weeks spent on the ice were full of activity.

The Inuit had accepted my presence among them, and that I had learned to survive and live among them, no more, no less. No trophies were offered for valour or courage. Eventually, when I was preparing for my return south, my friend who had invited me in for tea and had led the hunt and given me my Inuit name, asked me why I was leaving. I could only speak from my head, not my heart.

"I have to," I said.

In my heart, I knew that in spite of having had a positive experience in the community, I could not remain a single man there indefinitely, living like any "normal" person, and also be myself. Nor could I become a priest and be assured that I would return to this community, and even if I did, the isolation and not ever being among others like me would have been too difficult. So, all of my concerns went into that simple response: "I have to."

I wiped the tears from my eyes as I boarded the plane. As we ascended, the community disappeared quickly from view, but to this day I can visualize every person and every corner of the community. And though there were no trees, I still felt God's presence in the incredible beauty of the natural world and the varied wildlife.

I experienced a way of life that even then was rapidly disappearing. Climate change, social influences from the south, government policy, and a generation of Inuit losing touch with their culture have altered the Arctic forever. We've all seen films and talked to people who've been up there where that dotted line called the Arctic Circle crosses the map of Canada. But most of us don't know, "The People" or their land. I was blessed in having the opportunity to know both.

3

The
Priesthood

Ordination

*U*pon my return to Winnipeg in August, a local priest approached and asked me to help him out.

"I've just been made principal of a junior high school," he said, "and wondered if you would be interested in teaching religious studies to Grade 7-9 students."

"That's just in a few weeks!" was my startled reply, but I accepted the offer, grateful because it would give me the opportunity to work with youth before ordination. I knew I would have trouble defending certain teachings of the church that I wasn't too comfortable with myself and, sure enough, at one of the first classes, a student asked, "If God is unconditional love, why would he condemn us to hell for missing mass on Sunday?"

"Couldn't agree more with you," I thought to myself, but replied, "I understand... but the church teaches that it is a mortal sin to miss mass on Sunday."

It was an inadequate and transparent answer that was met with indifference and a hesitant smile.

Not long after getting re-settled in the city, the Chancellor of St. Boniface asked if I would consider being ordained for the Diocese of St. Boniface? He wanted to be supportive but he also wanted to keep me in the province.

"Thanks," I said, "but I'm rather uncomfortable with the tension between the English and French in this diocese."

"If you would like to meet with the Archbishop of Winnipeg to discuss the matter, let me arrange a meeting with him," he replied.

I knew he had my interest at heart so I agreed. The archbishop at the time was Cardinal Flahiff, a distinguished looking man who had a gentle and humble presence about him. After hearing about my studies and pastoral experiences, he thanked me for coming and invited me to come back in a few days for more discussion. When I returned, he wasted no time getting to it.

"Ray," he said, "would you consider taking a year of studies at St. Augustine's in Toronto, it's affiliated with the University of Toronto where you will be taking some of your theology classes."

He explained that he felt it was important for me to take my last year of theology in English in order to become familiar with English terminology in scripture and better prepare me for presentation and celebration of the sacraments.

"Consider it," he continued, but he did not press me for an immediate response. "If you're in agreement, come back in a few days to fill out the forms and we'll make preparations for your stay at St. Augustine's."

I found my connection with nature while in Winnipeg at either the Assiniboine or St Vital Park. It was in Assiniboine Park near the city zoo that I walked long and pondered hard this latest development. The background sound of some of the zoo's resident exotic birds blended with the local varieties while a gentle breeze only slightly disturbed the leaves of the giant oak and elm trees towering above me.

"What a change!" I thought as I recalled the contrasting, treeless, yet equally spiritual Arctic terrain.

While enjoying the peace and tranquility of the park, one question kept coming to mind: *"Had my studies at Voluntas Dei and my pastoral experiences been to prepare me, not only go to the seminary in Ontario that I initially didn't want to attend, but also to become a diocesan priest, which I had also initially avoided?"*

I had no feeling of regret about not retuning to the Voluntas Dei Institute in Quebec. A lot had happened since I finished my studies there; I had moved on. What I felt was gratitude for the wonderful memories and experiences the institute had given me. In fact, I felt surprisingly good about the cardinal's offer and decided to phone home with my decision.

In those years, every time I phoned home Mom held her breath, hoping I would have news of plans to complete my studies and settle down. So when I called and said, "Mom, I've decided to return home," she responded as she had over the previous few years.

"Oh Ray," followed by a long, negative sigh.

"I don't mean I'm moving back *home*," I quickly added. "I mean I've been accepted to belong to the Archdiocese of Winnipeg and the bishop, who is Cardinal Flahiff, is sending me to St. Augustine's in Toronto for my last year of studies."

"Oh Ray," she repeated, with a lot more energy... but no sigh. "Wait till our parish priest hears about this."

St. Augustine's is a large institutional-looking, brown brick and stone building, distinguished by a massive cross atop a dome. The entranceway is huge, with a high, pillared approach to the doors. Entering for the first time felt rather surreal to me, knowing all of our previous parish priests and bishops at home had walked through the same entranceway as young men.

Inside, the wood-panelled walls, marbled floors, wide hallways, high ceilings, and a chapel that was larger than our whole church at home were impressive, indeed. Our individual rooms were larger than my apartment in Winnipeg had been.

While I was moving in, some of my neighbours dropped by to introduce themselves and to welcome me; a new group of friends was quickly made. One of them later became the bishop of my home town, and the dean at the time eventually became the Archbishop of Toronto and was later installed as a cardinal.

Canon Law, the church's regulation in regards to the sacraments, was among my studies that year, along with a course in liberation theology, which proved to be a major influence in my life because it made me aware of the struggles of the clergy in different parts of the world — priests who struggled to support the needs of their people — and the church hierarchy that didn't want priests involved in politics. I found it to be the most insightful course in revealing similarities and parallels with the need for justice that gay priests had themselves been facing.

We took classes in how to celebrate the various liturgies and in leading a community in worship. In practising to say mass, attention was given to posture, movement, gesture, articulation, and reverence. We practised hearing confession, conducting a funeral, and administering the sacrament of the sick, often referred to as the last rites. I found the classes practical as well as visually and creatively appealing.

Some seminarians were preparing to be priests in my home town; others had as their bishop the young priest who had spent a summer teaching me Latin.

At the time, I thought I was still the only one with the "secret" and was constantly asking God to help me repress my feelings. Yet, years later, a sexual scandal made the news media about all the homosexual activity that had been going on at St. Augustine's Seminary at the same time I was there. I was shocked because I hadn't been aware of it, nor had anyone ever spoken of it. What hurt me most was all the anguish I had put myself through thinking that I was the only seminarian who had had the thoughts and feelings I did while naively living in the midst of others who were, obviously, just like me.

After St. Augustine's I returned to Manitoba. My year of preparation for internship (1976-77) for being ordained as a deacon, which would then be the last step before final ordination into the priesthood, took place in a Winnipeg parish similar to the one I had spent time at in 1971, serving a Catholic and an Anglican community. One day, when my bishop was visiting, he came face to face with the Anglican priest, who excused himself for not knowing how to properly address a cardinal. My bishop extended his hand and said, "I was baptised George." I was impressed that despite his rank, he was able to maintain humility and humour.

As a child, I had been taught that the Catholic Church was the only true church, and wondered if those who taught and preached that actually believed it themselves. Working closely with other denominations marked the beginning of my questioning of our "differences", whether they were important or relevant, and if God really cared about such trivial distractions. The Anglicans I met were as devout, spiritual, faithful, and Christian as any Catholic.

I was a Catholic only because I had been born into a Catholic family. I had always seen all religious groups and faiths as no better and no worse than any other. Everyone had different beliefs and rituals but all had a love of God. I had always been aware that we, as Catholics, were different, but I never accepted that we were better, somehow holier or more pleasing to God.

The pastor of the parish was a pleasant young priest but his live-in housekeeper made her position clear.

"If you want anything in the kitchen, let me know," she said bluntly upon my arrival.

In other words, it might have been my home, but it was her kitchen, and she had a presence about her that forcefully said, "Don't cross me!"

At the time, the Manitoba Department of Education asked me to update its Arctic collection by working with graphic designers and scriptwriters to produce a slide documentary for elementary students. Entitled *Inuit - the People of Canada's Arctic,* it is still available through the department.

I lived in two different worlds, one of parish ministry and the other of document preparation; the latter offered me a distraction and diversion from parish appointments and meetings, which I appreciated as a "cause" outside of parish ministry. It was as if I needed one foot outside at all times in order not to leave an important part of myself completely behind.

As the time approached for my ordination, with a serious look on his face, the pastor asked me into his office.

"Ray, I want you to keep in confidence what I am about to say to you."

"Of course," I replied.

"I won't be able to attend your ordination and will be leaving the parish in a month," he said, much to my amazement. "I have asked to leave the priesthood (laicization) because I am engaged to be married."

He gave me a moment to catch my breath and continued. "I'm sorry to be telling you all this as you begin your ministry."

Oddly enough, I felt really happy for him, to have had the courage to move on in his life by embracing freedom and love. He was a kind and gentle person, and God had given him the greatest gift, the love of another, though others may not have expressed it that way. It certainly was an interesting way to begin my ministry — and prophetic!

As a deacon, I had the opportunity to get a better idea of what the priesthood would be all about. I was assigned to a neighbouring parish set in a wooded area along the Assiniboine River close to Assiniboine Park, a perfect setting for me as I prepared for ordination into the priesthood. The pastor there was only too happy to give me all the pastoral experience I needed as a deacon, in preparation for being on my own as a priest in a few months. He asked me to attend all parish meetings: administrative, liturgical, catechetical, social and outreach.

Presiding over baptisms, weddings and funerals that didn't have a mass included required preparing three to five meetings with couples before their wedding or having a child baptized. Meetings with the family were held before a funeral for spiritual support and to help arrange the service according to any specific requests, which had to conform to diocesan regulations. Conducting the wake service before the funeral came next, then presiding at the funeral itself, and the interment, attending the reception, and then follow-up support of the family a few days later.

Funerals were quite involved, powerful, spiritual experiences for everyone involved, including me. As the saying goes, it's not over till the paperwork is done, so certificates and registry information had to be filled in and appropriately filed.

As for weddings, many couples were not comfortable with all of the things the church, through me, was asking of them. Besides all the preparation classes, they were encouraged to attend church more regularly and to have their children raised in the Catholic faith. Many attended merely to "get done," as the expression goes. Even before becoming a priest, though I enjoyed meeting the couples involved, I found myself becoming demanding for what the church was asking of them, and began taking their indifference and lack of enthusiastic commitment personally. I had heard priests talk with cynicism and an air of self- righteousness about these "pick-and-choose" Catholics, and I seemed to be developing into one of them.

"Hi Mom, it's Ray..." I paused and, in anticipation, she said nothing. "I have the date for my ordination."

"Oh Ray," she said with excitement and, I think, some disbelief.

"The bishop notified me that it will be May 19, 1978, at St. Paul the Apostle Church in Winnipeg."

When the day came, my family and an uncle were present, along with many priests, who were there to show their support and fraternity. A group of young people with lively and uplifting voices and the music of guitars, flutes, tambourines, and a keyboard offered powerful energy and emotion that accompanied a beautiful religious celebration led by Cardinal Flahiff.

My family was impressed and relieved that the date that had been anticipated since 1964, had finally arrived. Like a wedding, all I had to say was "I do" but, unlike a wedding, I went to bed alone that night. I had fantasized about a few men in the parish but my succumbing to the desire to be "more than friendly" was avoided for fear of being discovered and outed.

Parish Ministry

My first assignment as an ordained priest was to serve as assistant pastor at St. Augustine of Canterbury Church in Brandon. Although the pastor was well-liked and respected locally, somehow my relationship with him immediately took on tones reminiscent of the relationship I had had with my mother — getting along was a challenge.

Early on he was anxious for me to do something with the youth in his parish as soon as I, a newly ordained priest, arrived in the city. As well, a young nun, who was also just starting out in the religious life, was anxious to speak to the newly ordained priest in the parish. She was a delightful, energetic person, and she had a cause. She wanted to introduce me to a program for teens called "Search". Her enthusiasm and conviction kept my attention and the more she spoke about it the more interested I became.

It would be a highly active program, a live-in weekend retreat involving the teens themselves, chaperoned by three couples who would also be giving talks and be involved in a number of other activities. A great deal of planning, preparation and, of course, money were needed, but the Sister had done her homework and knew how successful the program had already been everywhere it had been given. With manuals detailing every activity, a list of talks prepared and financial needs laid out, we agreed to meet again to plan a strategy. Every step was accompanied by prayer.

In time, with a detailed outline of the program in hand, we met with the pastor to ask for permission to present the program to the parish committee, which, at the time, included the finance committee. Unfortunately, the pastor didn't share our excitement but said he would pass the idea on to the bishop for approval. He made it very clear that it was his parish and any project would only take place with his input and blessing.

Word spread that we were planning a live-in teen retreat. Calls started coming in and we lay low waiting for Sunday when we knew the pastor would get blasted with questions from parishioners. On Monday he called me into his office and gave his blessing to the project. I told him I was happy that the bishop had given it his blessing as well, knowing the bishop would be informed as soon as I left his office. But in order to have the last word, as I was leaving his office, the pastor reminded me that I needed to keep him informed.

Sixty participants attended our first Search weekend. It was such a success that we had a waiting list for another one. I was attracted by the free spirit of the young people, their vitality, energy and openness. Some saw themselves as "committed" even though they didn't attend Sunday services on a weekly basis. They would follow in their parents' footsteps when the need for the "rites of passage" came along.

They knew that if they didn't attend religious studies they would not get "done" and were apprehensive about what the emotional consequences of that might be. In response, some acted out, withdrew, became aloof, sarcastic or overly opinionated. They had to conform to fit in and be accepted and that frustrated them immensely. I could relate!

Though I had encountered one young man in his early 30s in our Search group to be sexually appealing, I could never fathom the idea of seducing him, nor any other man that appealed to me because I still believed I was the only Catholic male living with the fantasies that I had.

Ministerial meetings of all the Christian clergy and leaders of other faiths, a new experience in my personal ministry, were held monthly in Brandon to discuss issues of social and moral concern in the community, and to see if, as a faith community, we could have input in supporting charities and social agencies. We also sought to be supportive of one another as faith leaders. Many maintained a respectful distance and were reserved while among their colleagues.

I found an important fraternity and support in ministerial groups but it wasn't long before I saw the different denominations and "Christian groups", of which there are several hundred, as independent business groups that were protective and self righteous about their beliefs and their requirements for membership. The Catholic

Church — from my perspective — was certainly among them, no worse and no better than any of the others.

My friend Jim, a young, charismatic, energetic, and open-minded evangelical minister, was over visiting one day when he said he had to leave to get ready for his ministerial meeting.

"What do you mean, *your* ministerial meeting?" I asked with surprise, knowing he attended the same ministerial meetings that I did and I knew nothing of a scheduled meeting that day. "The evangelical ministers have their own ministerial group," he replied.

"Are you telling me there are two Christian ministerial groups in this city?" I continued in disbelief.

"Yes, it's for Christian ministers who can publicly say they accept Jesus Christ as their personal Lord and Saviour."

"And you believe the rest of us can't?" I asked. "No one ever asked me."

I was dismayed that this sort of thing actually existed, which only emphasized the rift that already existed among Christian churches.

"So," I went on, "if I were to publicly say to your group that I accept Jesus Christ as my personal Lord and Saviour, I could join?"

Jim looked at me with a wide smile, realizing I was game to do it, and said, "I don't see why not."

"Good," I blurted. "I'm going to change and I'll go with you... Are you alright with that?"

"This will be interesting," he responded.

"If you don't mind picking me up so I don't have to walk in alone?" I added.

"My pleasure," he said. "I'll pick you up in half an hour." Thirty minutes later, I walked out in my black, three-piece suit with Roman collar and cuffed sleeves.

Jim laughed as I got into his car. "I can't wait to see their faces," he said.

We walked into a group of about a dozen men and women who, when they looked at me, went completely stoic. Most of them already knew me from the mainstream ministerial to which they also belonged. We took our places around the table and the chairperson acknowledged my presence. Thanking him, I bluntly broke the ice.

"I'm aware that to be present in this group I need to acknowledge my acceptance of Jesus Christ as my personal Lord and Saviour, which I do."

The immediate tension and ill ease in the room was palpable.

"Thank you for your declaration," the chairperson responded while the others sat stunned and obviously annoyed.

After the meeting, during hot coffee and a cool reception from one and all, I said to Jim, "If we can't have respect and acceptance among ourselves, then it's a good indication that the process of healing the divisions within the Christian faith has a long way to go to reach what was said of Jesus' followers: 'See how they love one another',"

He nodded in agreement.

The wave I created that day was no tsunami, but perhaps it was challenging enough for a good surf.

In Brandon, I was often rejuvenated by God's presence at a nearby park where I was almost instantly calmed, comforted and strengthened. Many of the friends I met in those early days after my ordination remained a part of my entire priesthood. I became a part of their family fabric and they came to know a great deal about me — except my secret with God. Yet, out of my loneliness and insecurity, I had tremendous trouble in Brandon, particularly with the pastor.

I had managed to keep my anger with him pent-up inside for two years before it came to a head one day as I was putting on my vestments to say mass. The pastor came up to me and sternly complained, "Ray make sure no lights are left on after mass."

"Now, he's treating me like the caretaker," I thought.

But before I could even suggest the church caretaker take care of such things, he continued.

"And make sure the doors are all locked as well."

Then he stood, staring at me, waiting for some sign that I would obediently comply.

I wanted to let it go and just tell him his timing was terrible, that this was not the time to discuss trivial matters, or anything at all. I needed to prepare myself for mass in just a few minutes, but he didn't seem to care; he regularly intruded into my space at will, and I was always intimidated and afraid of confrontation. This was my first assignment as an ordained priest and he was my superior. What was I to do?

Well, this time something snapped! It was like he had thrown a lit match on gasoline. I lost my ability to think rationally.

"Damn!" I said under my breath, glaring at him with all the intensity and resentment I could muster. If looks could kill, I would have slain the man that very moment. I found myself breaking through that wall between us.

Livid, I stripped my mass vestments off and flung them at him as he stood and stared back at me in shock.

"You have a mass to say!" he yelled. "What are you doing?"

"No!" I fired back, barely able to control my anger and trembling body. "You have a mass to say! I'm out of here!" I turned and wanted to run right through the door.

"The bishop will be in touch with you!" I told him as I slammed the door behind me.

I gathered some personal items in the rectory and drove to Winnipeg. I must have stopped for gas at least, but all I can remember of that drive to the city is the dividing line on the highway.

A few years previous, friends in Winnipeg had told me that if I ever needed help to call on them. As I crossed the Perimeter Highway into the city, that invitation played in my mind as if it had just been offered.

It was late evening when Jake opened the front door of his house to see me standing there like a stray cat, suitcase in hand. His face told me he could sense that something was very wrong the instant he lay eyes on the wreck that I was.

"Ray?" he said tentatively, as I slowly entered and he took my coat. "You wanna go downstairs and rest?"

"Thanks Jake," I said as I felt my throat tighten and my eyes water.

"Is there someone I should call?"

"Call Father Dominique," I said.

We went downstairs and I parked myself on the couch in his basement family room. Jake and Wanda had lived in the same house for several years with their son Chris. It was a modest bungalow in the St. James area of west Winnipeg with four bedrooms, a full bathroom upstairs and downstairs and a half bath near the entrance. Along with a living room, dining room and kitchen on the main floor, there was a fully furnished basement that served as a recreation area with a TV, ping-pong and pool tables, and a small bedroom for visitors and drop-ins like myself. A two car garage was attached to the home.

"The bedding and towels in the bathroom are all clean," Jake said. "I'll leave you to it... we can talk in the morning."

I said nothing. It all seemed so surreal. I was in a state of disbelief as I moved about like some kind of zombie, getting the bedding out, undressing, doing bathroom duties, trying to make myself comfortable on the couch. I was dead tired and should have been able to sleep on a bed of nails, but as I replayed the scene with the pastor over and over, my anxiety grew into gut-wrenching fear, of what I wasn't sure, but sleep eluded me.

After a fitful night, I got up early the following morning and showered, got dressed and went upstairs to find Father Dominique sitting at the kitchen table with the family.

"Morning Ray... how are you?" he asked, obvious concern in his voice.

"Scared," I said as I sat down next to him as he poured me a cup of coffee. "I don't know what to do. I feel like hiding somewhere for awhile."

Chris had been listening from across the table. "Father Ray, you could stay with some of my friends," he said. His parents turned to him in disbelief.

"Chris, Father Ray is not one of your hippie friends," Jake said.

"How do think your friends will feel about a depressed priest staying with them?" I asked him. And as the words came out of my own mouth I felt the tears welling up in my eyes. I wanted to scream and cry and simply disappear in the utter hopelessness that I would ever find someone with whom to share the aching hurt of my loneliness and frustration.

"I'll just tell them you're a friend who needs a place to stay, a guy who needs to be left alone for awhile," he replied confidently, his mouth full of Cheerios. "And if you pay for your room and board, they won't ask questions."

"Sounds like you have some nice friends," I said, taking another sip of comforting hot coffee.

"They're just a group of people who decided to move in together to support each other in taking care of the house they rent. It's not a four-star hotel; they'd probably give you the spare room in the basement with nothing but a mattress on the floor."

I thanked Chris and decided to give it a shot. I had to stay somewhere. Jake offered the basement family room for as long as I needed it, if I wanted it, but we all seemed to know instinctively that I'd be more comfortable at arm's length from close acquaintances. I asked Chris if he would take me over to meet his friends.

After breakfast, we all talked a short while longer, then Jake and Wanda left for work before Chris took me to his friends' house, a huge rambling, three-storey near the Assiniboine River in the Wolseley area of the city. I was taken downstairs and shown my room, which, as Chris had warned, consisted of a closet, a mattress on the floor, and a small window high on the south wall. Thankfully, Chris's parents had supplied me with bedding, towels and blankets.

I met a few more of the young tenants in the kitchen of the big house but I don't remember any of their faces nor, for that matter, the food they offered me, nor any other details about the house. The clearest memories I have of my few weeks on that mattress are of my bedside companion — the house cat —- and how exhausted and emotional I felt the whole time.

Father Dominique had been a well-respected Oblate Father who was also a trained psychologist. He was retired but he was an old friend and more than willing to visit me daily. He gave me paper and a pen to journal with, and then on subsequent visits he would listen to me share my written ramblings. I wrote often, long and furiously; it flowed out of me as if from a bursting damn.

Father Dominique told me he would support my taking time away from the parish and would assure the bishop, Cardinal Flahiff, that I was safe and would appreciate money for room and board to support my hosts. Later, he told me the cardinal wanted to assure me of his prayers and best wishes.

I got up whenever I awoke but spent most of my days in my dark little room sleeping, crying or writing. My daily prayer, which I would say several times, went like this: "Dear God, I don't know what has happened to me or how long this will last, but I know that you are caring for me and that I will be okay."

One evening toward the end of my stay in Woleseley, I was out for a walk when I suddenly became very frightened that I might meet someone on the street, anyone! I had never experienced anything like that before and, sure enough, I soon spotted someone coming towards me and was filled with anxiety. I quickly crossed the street to avoid him and made it to the corner, then back home without actually coming face to face with anyone. The whole experience made me aware of just how weak and vulnerable I had become.

Until that evening, I had always enjoyed the streets in the area. Many of them are thickly lined on both sides with large elm trees, their branches reach over the sidewalks to touch each other in the middle, forming a protective green canopy over the street and the people below.

"Alone with myself
The trees bend to caress me
The shade hugs my heart."
— Candy Polgar

After the fearful walk, I was exhausted and needed to sleep. Without invitation, the cat curled up next to my head and we closed our eyes. This quickly became a part of our routine habit any time I would lay down to rest. A few days later, as I awoke from one such escape from reality, with my furry friend very near my head, my gaze was drawn to the small window. Outside, I could see the bright blue sky and for some reason, felt filled with a new energy, like a new person. It was as if I had been in a deep coma for a long time. I looked around in dismay that I had slept on that mattress on the floor for almost a month. I felt compelled to leave.

I got up and thanked those of my hosts who were present and said goodbye to the cat, which had been my constant companion. He had literally been a godsend, a guardian for this human, a creature that could sense my dis-ease and instinctively give comfort, almost healing, with his intimate, undemanding presence. And, like most cats, when he sensed that I had been healed, he did as most cats do and ignored me.

Before my stay with Chris's friends, I had never experienced young people who would offer such hospitality to a stranger, with no conditions, expectations or comment, other than a few words of gratitude for my financial support. I knew, as I left their home, that my time with them and their cat had been a spiritual experience. They were not, by any means, religious, but they had been very spiritual in their compassion and hospitality. I believed that they found great favour with God and that they hadn't needed to be religious to earn that favour. That was an epiphany for me.

I had asked Cardinal Flahiff for a transfer away from Brandon and, unknown to me, he had been approached by Sister Viola, a pioneer in ministry with the Deaf, and totally committed.

She had asked the cardinal for a priest to help her offer pastoral care to the hundreds of families with a member, and sometimes every individual in the family, who was deaf. She asked for an energetic and expressive priest that could help her develop a parish community — Church of Silence. Guess who the cardinal had in mind!

"Ray," he said, "if you're willing to accept Sister Viola's request you'll be sent to study at Gallaudet College in Washington D.C. and stay at Immaculate Conception Parish on Massachusetts Avenue. You will earn your stay by helping out with their parish masses."

Excited about the proposal, I immediately asked, "When do I leave?"

"In a few days," he replied. The last time I had been told that I would be leaving in a few days, I found myself heading for the Arctic. This experience would be far from that, but once again, the idea of doing something outside the status quo, away from the unhappiness of my "usual" life, gave me a feeling of freedom and exhilaration.

The residence on Massachusetts Avenue was like a small estate, with five assistant priests, a cook, a housekeeper, a sacristan, and someone taking care of the property. On the same property were an elementary school, a parish hall, and an administration building. The parish supported a few charities and a few less fortunate black parishes.

"Welcome Ray," the pastor said with a wide smile upon my arrival. "I suggest you get to sleep early since starting tomorrow morning you'll be saying the 6 a.m. weekday masses."

Of course, mass at 6 a.m. marked the beginning of my day — well before breakfast. I was quite surprised to see over 100 people at each mass, along with a choir of five well-paid professional singers. For the most part, the attendees were professional people starting their day with prayer.

Typically, when I returned to the residence for breakfast before heading to the university, I entered a long dining room with priests scattered around a huge table reading their papers and eating their breakfasts. Once in awhile someone would comment on what they were reading, otherwise they read and ate silently, with a local radio channel playing in the background.

"Good morning Father, what would you like for breakfast," I was asked as I sat down and was handed a newspaper. "And how would you like it prepared?"

After breakfast, I took a standing-room-only bus to the university, surrounded by men in three piece suits in the heat of summer, standing there looking comfortable while I was sweating in a short-sleeved shirt.

"What deodorant are these guys using?" I often wondered.

After getting off the bus at Dupont Circle, I caught a subway to the campus. During the regular school year, several thousand students at the college used sign language. I arrived as one of a few thousand summer students, a beginner, who could communicate only in English. Once again, as when I was among the Inuit, I felt isolated and disconnected, but accepted. The contrast to my Brandon experience was not lost on me. Everyone was so expressive I could often piece together what they were talking about by their body language and facial expressions.

I managed to get through the beginner and intermediate programs in the three months I spent in Washington. My stay was a privileged experience that offered me insight into a very wealthy class of people who often used their gifts and resources to help many people.

Having touched the edge of the world of those in power and influence in Washington, and the world of those who lived in silence at the college was an important part of my spiritual journey.

But then the call came from Winnipeg and I never got the opportunity to use sign language again.

"Ray, this is the bishop; I need you to return to Winnipeg as soon as possible," he said with a sense of urgency.

"Father Ted has had a severe heart attack and needs immediate attention and rest... you're the only priest we have available to replace him."

"I'm sorry to hear that," I replied. "I will make immediate arrangements."

In the priesthood, changes often came quickly and it was my duty to be available and ready. My personal preferences as a person were secondary to the needs of the church.

Having a few hours before my flight, and knowing I wouldn't get a meal on the plane, which would be arriving late, I found a counter with a variety of take-out food. I purchased an exotic drink, a large deli sandwich loaded with everything, a decadent dessert, and looked for a table. Outside, near a ramp to a car park, I saw a small manicured piece of lawn with a few small willows and a picnic table. I headed for it through the nearest exit, dodging other travellers and on-coming traffic outside. I claimed the picnic table and spread out my bounty.

With traffic steadily passing by and people walking up and down the ramp nearby, there on my patch of heaven God's presence filled me with absolute bliss. I had two hours to enjoy the grass, the blue sky, and the gently swaying willows before heading back to my boarding gate.

With my banquet before me and nature's magnificence around me, with the backdrop of a busy international airport, I was very aware of how God's presence could be experienced, though not always easily, in the midst of anything. While savouring every morsel of food, sip of my drink, and the warm breeze, I gave thanks to God. Full of hope, I was ready for Canada and a new experience of parish ministry in a place called Winnipegosis, Manitoba.

I was in cattle country almost immediately after crossing the north Perimeter Highway beyond the Winnipeg city limits, heading north. What else could you use land for that is dotted with marshes, huge rocks, and soil that is minerally challenged? An hour had passed and, except for the occasional field of grain or sunflowers, the scenery had not changed. I passed small villages that were well out of sight behind me within the count of ten. The farther I travelled into the land of the moose, elk, and bear, the more road kills I saw on the highway and its shoulders.

Approaching three hours out of the city, I came upon the fair-sized community Dauphin, with lots of stores and more than one gas station. But half an hour later, I was again travelling down a corridor of highway lined with fir trees until a large lake appeared, Lake Winnipegosis, which was so large I couldn't see the other side.

Then, out of nowhere, appeared the Village of Winnipegosis, where I was to be pastor of five communities composed primarily of people of Polish background. I was reminded of my days at the seniors' centre in Winnipeg. Many Ukrainians and Mennonites also lived in the village, and a number of aboriginal communities were nearby. Most of the people were descendants of hard working settlers, strong in their cultures and traditions. To change anything was difficult for them.

The Catholic Church, which held about 200 people, was well kept, in large part because of the efforts of the local church ladies' group and six Benedictine Sisters, who also ran the community hospital. The Sisters played the organ on Sundays, led the choir, supported the ladies' group, and knew everyone in town. Before long, I became extremely grateful for their support and friendship. Their main religious community and retreat house were just north of Winnipeg and became like a second home for me as well. I always felt welcome there, as did anyone else seeking a retreat.

Interwoven into almost all aspects of the community, the Sisters were often my source of sanity and encouragement. I was also very grateful to their cook, who was constantly baking and preparing beautiful meals; I jumped at every invitation to partake. They also had a huge garden, which I not only benefited from as a source of fresh produce, but also as a place of solace.

Church services were always well attended and parishioners were uncommonly active in catechism programs that we introduced for their children. Parish and finance committees were set up in each community, and ladies groups raised money from annual "fall suppers", rummage and bake sales.

Parishioners kept my freezer full. The men supplied me with all kinds of wild meat, ducks and fish; the women kept me full of pastries, deserts and other goodies, as well as full homemade dinners.

Winnipegosis was a commercial fishing community, which gave me the opportunity once a week to go out on a fishing boat, and net me my fill of pickerel. We would leave at 4 a.m. and return at 4 p.m.

Sometimes the boats would get close to each other and the language at times would be rather crude. The men on my boat enjoyed warning those on the other boat.

"You should be careful of your language, we have your pastor on board."

Of course their own language wasn't much better and everyone had a good laugh.

> "The woods were made for the hunters of dreams,
> The brooks for the fishers of song;
> To the hunters who hunt for the gunless game
> The streams and the woods belong."
> — Sam Walter Foss

My second parish, in Pine River, was farther to the northwest and a half-hour drive through a thick forested area that seasonally attracted hunters from far and wide looking for moose, black bear and elk.

The people of Pine River took great pride in their homes and properties. The ladies' group was well organized and the craft and bake sales were crowd pleasers. I recall one elderly lady who was losing her sight, yet she made hand-crocheted tablecloths that were really fine art. In larger centres, they could have been sold as such, full of precise detail, the culmination of hours of loving work over several months. When I left the community, she gave me one of her tablecloths as a gift, which I will never part with. It represented what she could not say to me in words, like the care packages that Mom used to mail to me at Christmas.

The ladies kept the parish viable and were friends and a support for each other through times of joy and difficulty. They were an amazing group of women.

Ethelbert, another of my parishes, was half an hour's drive west of Winnipegosis. If you were not Polish in this community you were considered an outsider, and the priest was no exception. Perhaps it was a good thing that being an "outsider" was not new to me.

The parish was run by two families that were related and entrenched in Polish customs and religiosity. The church was small and rustic, holding about 100 people. A wood stove was situated in the middle of the aisle. The three altar boys, Paul, Mike and Peter, were in their late teens and as tall as me, and quite hilarious. My organist, Dan, was a young Ukrainian friend of theirs and the four of them kept me sane with their youthful antics. I met Dan again in October, 2000, at his world premiere musical, *The Strike,* about the 1919 Winnipeg general strike.

The little church was full and the people were dressed in their finest at my first Easter service in Ethelbert. A Polish elder, who was the church patriarch, was smiling at me before the service, I guessed, to make sure we were on good terms. As we prepared for the service in the sacristy just off the main sanctuary, Paul, Mike, Peter and Dan decided to hand me a letter saying that they were going on strike for higher pay.

"I don't give you guys anything," I told them in disbelief.

"That's our point," Paul said. "We would like some of what you will receive today."

Knowing that I would probably get a few dollars as gifts, I agreed. But they knew something I didn't, which, of course, was the basis of their whole hidden agenda.

Just before the scrvice, the patriarch came into the sacristy to tell me that Jesus was lying in front of the altar.

"*Who* is lying in front of the altar?" I asked, bewildered.

One of the young con artists spoke up to tell me a statue of Jesus lying in the tomb was always placed in front of the altar before Easter mass. I had to go and wave the incense smoke over it, sprinkle it with holy water, and say a few words, after which the cons would say "Amen" and we would return to the sacristy. So out we went, and sure enough, there it was. I did my thing, and we returned.

The patriarch came back and asked me to wait for a few minutes. The cons were smiling a lot.

"Jesus is now on the altar," the patriarch said upon his return, then quickly returned to the sanctuary.

"He was dead a minute ago and now he's on the altar?" I asked the cons, who could hardly contain themselves.

"They took the dead Jesus out and put a statue of the resurrected Jesus on the altar," Mike explained.

I did my thing again, they said "Amen", and we returned to the sacristy.

"Are there any more statues?" I asked.

"No," Peter said, "but you're going to have to look at the back side of that one for the next forty days."

Finally, the mass began and everything was going along well until the collection. The patriarch marched towards me carrying the collection basket and handed it to me.

"Why are you giving this to me?" I quietly asked him with a forced smile.

"It's our custom," he said, adding, "At Easter, you have to pass the first collection."

I looked at the cons.

"It's the custom," Peter repeated with a shrug.

The whole congregation was looking bewildered to see that I didn't seem to know what was going on. I got up with my basket in hand and Dan played the organ like a pro. I went from pew to pew, smiling and thanking everyone as they put money into the collection plate. It took me a few minutes to manoeuvre with my vestments on but, finally, it was over and I sat down while the ushers took the second collection.

After mass, the patriarch came back to the sacristy to tell me they would need a few minutes to prepare things.

I looked at the cons, and asked, "What things?"

"They are going to get some Easter baskets of food for you to bless," Mike said, "then we go back out and sprinkle water on a few of them."

The cons knew very well that when we went back into the sanctuary everyone in the church would have a huge basket full of food. I thought I could bless the crowd with one symbolic sprinkling for all, but no, the custom was for every one of them to come up to have their basket individually blessed with holy water. Where the cons were getting all the holy water and I dared not ask.

Finally, back in the sacristy I thought it was over when the patriarch came again, thanked me, and ceremoniously handed me the collection I had personally taken.

"This is for you," he said with a smile of satisfaction.

"What do you mean, for me?" I repeated, again in disbelief.

"It's our custom that the first collection at Easter is for the priest and his needs."

I thanked him and he left, then the cons approached me with wide anxious smiles.

"A deal's a deal" they chorused. "And without us you would have been lost," Peter added, not realizing the larger truth of his words because those boys were truly a comfort to me, even though I'm sure some of them have since served time.

One year, word got out that it would be nice to have a large Christmas tree in the church in Winnipegosis. A few weeks before Christmas, one of my young friends came over to tell me he and some friends had just put a tree up in the church and I should go see it. Indeed, a huge tall tree stood to the side of the altar at the front of the church. It was massive and perfectly shaped.

"Where did you get it?" I asked in amazement.

"A donation," he said.

That same day, the police came over to ask me if anyone had spoken to me about a tree that had been cut down and taken in the night from a Ukrainian woman's property.

"No," I answered truthfully. "No one has come to speak to me about that."

There were a lot of suspicious looks in church the following Sunday morning — at both the tree and at me.

"An anonymous donation," was all I could say.

After one of the church services in Pine River, a quite short, elderly man wearing a suit that was likely in fashion in some much earlier era, asked to speak with me. People seemed happy to see him, though he rarely came to church and was rarely seen in the village.

"Do you have time to come over to my home today?" he asked.

I had a few hours before leaving for my next parish so I said, "Yes, I do."

"What are you driving?" he asked.

"A Ford, LTD, four-by-four half ton," I replied.

"Good, follow me," he said.

I had no idea where we were going as we drove north out of the village. Several miles later, without a crossing road or driveway anywhere in sight, he turned his signal light on and headed for the ditch.

"Where is he going," I muttered to myself.

As I slowed down to follow him off the road, a tire-track path could be seen leading into the woods. Tree branches hit my truck as we went farther and farther into the bush. Finally, we came to a beautiful clearing.

"Wow! I don't believe this!" I said.

In front of me was an authentic log cabin with a rustic front porch. Beside the cabin was a large enclosed corral with horses, cows, pigs, sheep, goats, chickens, geese, and a mule. It looked like the roundup for Noah's Ark, but no large boat was in sight. A little farther to the west was another coral with double log-rail fencing that sagged between rotting posts.

The entire homestead was situated at the edge of a very large valley. Across the valley I could see high hills, or what I came to know as "Manitoba mountains". It was autumn and the panoramic view of the valley and the hills beyond in all their brilliant colours was truly spectacular.

We got out of our vehicles and the old guy invited me into the cabin. There was no electricity so he lit a lamp and I felt like I had stepped into another era. The cabin consisted of one large room, a few small windows, wooden shelves, a wooden table and chairs, a cot and clothes on pegs at strategic spots on the walls. Piles and piles of National Geographics, all of which he had read, were everywhere. There was no toilet in sight in the house so I knew where it likely was.

"May I give you something to drink?" he asked.

"Yes, thank you," I said.

As he took a white cup from a hook on the wall, passed a cloth over it, removed the lid of a 45-gallon drum and submerged the cup into it, I quickly asked, "A drink of what?"

As soon as he had taken the lid off the drum, the smell of pine needles was almost overwhelming. He just smiled slightly as he handed me the cup. I was about to have my first full cup of pine-needle wine and I knew that it would have a very high alcohol content and with one sip I would be in trouble. I nursed it along very slowly, like champagne, but champagne it was not.

The old man was very kind and gentle, soft spoken and appeared to be in good health. He reminded me of my father in many ways. My father would have thought he was in heaven had he seen the cabin and its idyllic setting, and he would have liked this old gentleman.

"How long have you lived here?" I asked him.

"Sixty years," he replied.

As we sipped our wine, he explained that he had begun to settle the property in his twenties. He was married at the time but his wife died shortly after and he never remarried. He never mentioned children and I didn't ask. He said he knew of a few other men who lived like he did, as hermits. Some had since died and, he said, he would soon join them.

"What do you mean?" I asked.

"That's why I asked you to come here, Father. I want to tell you what I am about to do, and would like to ask you to deliver this letter when I am gone." He handed me an envelope. "As a priest," he said, "I know that I can trust you, and I would like you to do this for me."

"How can I help?" I asked.

"We know when we are about to die," he continued. "After we have settled our affairs, we go into those hills you see on the other side of the valley... and go into a cave that we have prepared for ourselves. We enclose ourselves and wait for our last breath."

In silence, we sipped the last of our wine.

"In a month," he continued, "if the people in the village haven't heard from me, give this letter to the police. Tell them that I entrusted it to you... no more than that."

I nodded in agreement.

In a matter-of-fact tone, as if he were talking about the weather, he said, "I will give my animals away before I leave. I believe in God and I know that He will care for me. I have had a good life and I have been very happy here... but it's time for my life here to end."

Feeling privileged to be in his trust, yet sad knowing that this would be the only time we would see each other, I listened to him share parts of his life story as we finished our drinks. Afterward, we wished each other God's peace and I left him. Two months later, a parishioner told me that people were looking for the old man. I immediately took his letter to the police.

That humble man had been living a very spiritual life with his God; there was no doubt in my mind about that. He had not asked for the last rites or for me to hear his confession, nor had I offered them. As far as I was concerned, this man didn't need them. He had been living in heaven and would continue to do so.

While in Winnipegosis, I befriended the Mennonite minister and we maintained contact for many years. Dan was an enthusiastic young married man with a family. He had a strong faith and a love of life. He spoke to everyone in the community no matter what denomination they were, and he was respected and loved by his Mennonite community, and by my Catholic one as well.

Dan was always very supportive of young parishioners who wanted to attend a Bible college. He said that many young people, after attending a Bible College, became more involved in their parish communities and some had considered parish ministries and even ordination.

"How odd that someone would be willing to take a year or two after high school to study the Bible," I thought.

"Bible studies" had been a Protestant concept to me since childhood, when we were discouraged from reading the Bible at home. What a great leap to the current generation that wondered why the Catholic Church didn't have Bible colleges. Even the young people in the Search program in Brandon had often asked, "Why don't Catholics have Bible Colleges like our non-Catholic friends do?"

I got some insight into what they would experience at a Bible college from our Search program, in which young people had opportunities to discuss scriptural passages, issues of moral and ethical concern for them, and to prepare liturgical celebrations. They learned to work as a team and to experience mutual support and encouragement. Being among their own peers they studied and discussed their faith in a non-threatening environment. It had a profound impact on all who experienced Search weekends. I could see how extending that experience over a year or two in a college environment could be life-altering for young people. For many Protestant students, such studies were a rite of passage.

So when a Catholic workshop was offered in Winnipeg on the topic of scriptural studies, I was immediately drawn to it. Those in attendance were concerned that their children did not have the same opportunity as non-Catholics to attend a Bible College. Since I had often spoken about the subject with Dan, the idea sparked a keen interest in me and I let it be known. That evening, a few of us met with the facilitator of the workshop.

While there had been a lot of interest, only those willing to make a commitment to meeting regularly were asked to meet after the workshop to pursue the notion of a Catholic Bible college. Five committed souls remained late into the evening, and we decided to meet again in two weeks. We took each other's names and phone numbers and agreed to reflect on our personal interest and commitment after receiving feedback from others about the concept, and on questions and concerns for future discussion.

"Wait till Dan hears about this," I thought to myself.

I had been asked if I would be willing to speak to the cardinal about what had come out of the workshop and to get his reactions before we went any further. I would then share his feedback at our next meeting. I called the cardinal right away and asked, "May I meet with you before returning to my parish concerning the workshop on scriptural studies?"

The cardinal, having been a scriptural scholar himself, welcomed my visit.

After telling him about our intended future meeting and the questions we would be discussing, he agreed to meet with me again after our next follow-up session. He seemed very happy about my enthusiasm and interest in the cause.

"May I have your blessing in pursuing this project?" I asked.

"Don't commit yourself without keeping me informed," he replied, and with that I returned to my parish.

The notion of scriptural studies became the topic of conversation with everyone I met in the parish. I gathered pages of input reflecting this considerable interest. The others in the group had similar experiences in their home communities and were equally well prepared for a lively follow-up session. When we got together, we were all anxious to talk, and all at the same time, so someone had to chair the meeting and someone else had to take notes.

Out of that meeting, with representation from Saskatchewan and Manitoba, developed what we called the "Catholic Bible College Interim Steering Committee". I accepted the chairmanship, alongside a Benedictine Sister from Winnipeg as secretary, and we began formulating a concept vision, goals, priorities, and a schedule for meetings.

"Before going any further, we need to prepare an outline I can present to the cardinal for his blessing," I reminded the group.

Then a member from the St Boniface Diocese reminded us that the City of Winnipeg had two dioceses within it and would require the blessing of both bishops. Then it was noted that within the Province of Manitoba, there are five dioceses. How were we going to get representation from all of them? On whose behalf were we speaking? And on what authority and with what credibility did the committee consider forming a Catholic Bible College?

We had some political logistics to work out. We needed to be well organized before discussing visions, concepts and all the related topics.

The cardinal informed us that a meeting of Western Canadian bishops was coming up and that he would like to notify them of what was being discussed and ask for feedback from them.

We sat on our hands while they met. When the cardinal returned from the meeting, he reported cautious interest within certain guidelines.

The bishops suggested that a steering committee be made up of representatives from each of the Western provinces and from the bishops, priests and laity. The cardinal agreed to keep the bishops informed.

We were overwhelmed with this development because we hadn't yet really started discussing anything in detail. But we forged ahead and asked that the bishops from each of the Western provinces choose a bishop who would be interested in attending monthly meetings. We also asked the Council of Priests to choose a representative and to provide representation from the laity. The steering committee would have a bishop, a priest, and at least two laypersons from each of the Western provinces and the Territories.

In addition, the cardinal could see that this would be a long- term project and would need administrative support so he offered our secretary an office in the chancery, which also gave him a close eye on developments. Within the next month we had stationery, a phone, and were ready to do mailings and updates.

We were offered the facilities at the Grey Nun Centre in Edmonton, Alberta, for our monthly meetings. The executive knew the topics and issues that needed to be discussed and we organized our meetings to maximize the time we had and to exhaust the topics as thoroughly as possible, taking into account all the considerations brought up in previous discussions.

Our secretary drew up the minutes, sent out updates, and made all the arrangements at the centre; all we had to do was show up on time. Each diocese made a great commitment in financially supporting our travel to Edmonton. The Sisters in Edmonton were great hosts and my own diocese was very supportive in offering the committee office space and a salary for our full-time secretary.

The months and years went by quickly. At the end of five years, the Bible college in Canmore, Alberta, opened. The vision had been to keep it as a "grassroots" college, meaning that it would be run for and by the laity with continued support and input from the church hierarchy. But in order to have the church's continued blessing, it became top heavy with hierarchy and bureaucracy. Within a few years it closed! All the efforts that had been put into the realization of a Catholic Bible College evaporated.

At the time, I couldn't understand why the church hierarchy could let something like that happen when there had been so much interest and support. The closure had a profound effect on me. Everything had been going along so well. The laity especially, had spent years and many, many hours doing ground work, researching, reporting, studying with sub-committees throughout their provinces, meeting with bishops and finance committees, even finding a suitable building and hiring a director from applications received from across Canada.

The hierarchy had allowed the laity and the clergy to do all the work but were determined to make it clear to everyone that it was "in charge". Once the vision of a grassroots structure was lost, it all came apart.

Dan had not only been instrumental in my getting involved in the Bible college project, as frustrating and disappointing as it was in the end, but also in much of my more positive experiences in Winnipegosis. Early one evening, near the end of my time there, he came over to invite me out for supper. I found it odd that we were not having the meal with his family, especially since his wife had been so supportive of our friendship. I also found it odd that he was wearing a suit, which he only did for church services.

When we walked into the restaurant, no one else was there. He quickly said there was a buffet in the back hall but I immediately became suspicious. He opened the door to allow me to enter first and there before me was his entire parish community, standing at their tables and giving me a standing applause. I could not hold back the tears.

They gave me a Catholic Bible that evening in which they had all signed their names inside the covers. I will always cherish that gift, along with the many signs of caring and cherished memories of so many God-loving people in the Winnipegosis Parish.

After having worked on the Catholic Bible College so long and hard, I was left with my five small communities to serve, but no trips and meetings to plan, no cause to promote. A huge void and silence within overtook me. I cried during the day but did not know why. As the days passed, I felt extremely lonely, and yet there were so many friends and parishioners that I could have visited.

My spirit yearned for connection, and for fulfillment as a gay male, for the sexual intimacy and companionship that the good people around me could never provide to a priest. I was trapped; a great part of my pain was in not being able to talk about my feelings, not being able to tell anyone my secret, which added to my isolation and loneliness. I needed a change.

I left Winnipegosis in 1985 to begin a new assignment in Dunrea and the surrounding four communities in southwestern Manitoba. I was hopeful, but with that move, a growing perception of having undue expectations placed upon me only heightened. It started almost immediately with the men's Catholic organization known as the Knights of Columbus, along with the church ladies groups and a few "pillars" of the church, who were accustomed to befriending the priest and assisting him in running the parishes.

When I arrived, the task before me seemed overwhelming, especially when I realized that those who had been running everything really didn't want changes while many others, including myself, did. The Knights were very active in all the parishes and were the main supporters of church activities and projects in the community. Since all the previous priests had been members of the Knights and I chose not to be, tension filled the air. They let me know that if I were a Knight, they were certain I would get much better co-operation and would feel much more included.

It wasn't long before the bishop invited me to come to see him. He wanted to know how things were going, though he already knew. After the usual fraternal hug and a friendly cup of coffee, he got to the point.

"I'm surprised to hear that you don't seem interested in being a member of the Knights," he said, then pointed out all the good work the Knights do and the sense of fraternity and support the group could offer me. "Perhaps you should give it further consideration," he added.

As often happened at such "cordial" visits, little consideration was given to what I did or didn't want, which only served to heighten my isolation.

In Dunrea a few days later, the main Knight dropped over to see how I was doing. Within a few minutes the invitation to join was once again extended to me and I accepted, realizing I really had no choice if I wanted the support in the community, which I needed. I felt I had sold my soul, and I had. I was caught between the expectations of the people and those of the bishop, with little support from either, and nowhere to turn.

Every parish had women who were seen as the "pillars" of the community. They prepared the children for the sacraments and when the children and their parents were prepared to be a part of the parish, the children received the sacraments. These "pillars" kept an eye on me to make sure I didn't move anything in the church or do anything without their opinion and permission. If I did, guess who they called?

Some families, who were not regular parishioners — seldom showing up at church or church functions - still wanted the "rites of passage" for their children. Some young couples wanted to get married in the church and yet were not actively practicing members of the parish. Parishioners would sometimes complain if I didn't hug all the children, or visit them as often as their previous pastor had done. I often found myself torn between the needs of those parishioners who were no longer attending regularly and the regulations of the church. I was uncomfortable with many of the expectations and regulations of the church that many parishioners did not want to follow, and which others could not follow, such as having to attend church regularly in order to avail themselves of its services. Mothers and grandmothers, for example, spoke of the pain of rejection by the church in not being allowed to have their children accepted for baptism unless they began coming to church more often.

But despite all the wrangling and criticism, the one constant enjoyable challenge was the meetings with young couples. I often saw myself in them, caught between the expectations of their parents and those of the priest. I secretly enjoyed their independent spirit; their seemingly rebellious outlook was refreshing, though I was often unable to provide them with the services they wanted without strings attached.

In preparing for marriage, they had often been pressured by their parents, and especially their grandparents, to get married in a Catholic Church. If left on their own, many couples would have been much happier with an outside, civil marriage, or for some, at least a hassle-free church wedding. Many parents and grandparents had an ingrained belief that unless one got married in a church, God wouldn't attend. With one in two marriages failing, every elderly Catholic grandmother was quick to explain why.

Couples wanting a church wedding knew what to do. They would show up for a few Sundays before asking to see me, making sure to greet me as they left the church. They would agree to everything I would ask of them, but the next time I saw them after the wedding would be when they had a newborn in their arms. And the cycle of getting the child "done" was passed on to a new generation.

But, in defense of these couples, they had not been given much of a choice. If they had been honest about their intentions to simply use the church for a public ceremony, which they would have wanted to arrange themselves, the following would have resulted: they would have been refused; then they would have been "labeled" by the institution as having been married "outside" the church, and therefore not in good standing with the institution; and they would have to live with that "guilt trip".

If I could get them to at least consider the possibility of going along with church requirements, I would give the green light to proceed, knowing that we would likely go through it all again when they returned with a child in their arms.

I felt very alone, isolated, and often at odds with the women pillars who faithfully followed the regulations of the church. And I was immensely bothered by those regulations because of how annoyed people could get in having to arbitrarily conform to them, and because of the implication that somehow God was connected with it all — that by "going along" with all the regulations, one was doing the Will of God and by inference, by not going along, one was somehow disobeying God.

In my view, God could not have cared less one way or the other. They were church, man-made regulations, and the only people who really cared about them were those working for the institution, which, as a priest, included me. Subconsciously, and as time went on, not so subconsciously, that conflict took its toll on me.

To say I was not happy with parish ministry would have been a gross understatement. I couldn't see things getting any better, no matter where they put me. Yet, the majority of people were very kind and understanding so, at one level, I didn't understand why I was going through so much turmoil. Why was I so unhappy? Why couldn't I settle down and stop taking things so much to heart? After all, as a parish priest, I had always lived a privileged lifestyle. My rent and food were always paid for and I had insurance, a pension and health benefits all under a diocesan plan. All my basic necessities were taken care of, the cost of which, for any of my parishioners, would take up the bulk of their wages.

In most of my parishes, someone else did my weekly housecleaning, receptionist duties and property mainte-nance. My only financial concerns were my car payments; even my gasoline bills were partially covered. Outside of scheduled appointments, I enjoyed the freedom to go on personal errands and private endeavours without waiting for scheduled days off. There was no such thing as fifteen-minute breaks and half-hour lunch periods.

I had so much going for me: security, respect, independence, health and hundreds of supportive people that I could visit. And if I needed anything, they would be there for me. But, despite all of that, a loneliness persisted. Reading, going for walks, watching TV, nothing seemed to satisfy my lonely spirit; I didn't know what to do to find peace.

With each passing year, feelings of being alone intensified and negatively affected my outlook on everything I did. Every day, my spirit quickly became drained of enthusiasm; the daily schedule became a tedious grind. I had only emptiness inside.

But my constant run-ins with the pillars of the communities, my refusal to be a more active member of the Knights, complaints to the bishop about something I had said in my homily, or about those I was visiting and those that I wasn't, had not held me in good standing with my superiors. I was becoming as demanding as others had been on me, paternalistic and patriarchal, full of negative energy, defensive, self-righteous and arrogant.

As always, I knew there was something different about me. I had kept my secret throughout my seminary studies and into my priesthood, never realizing that it was the most important gift of my life, the pearl that I needed to discover and disclose, and in doing so to find the connection and sexual intimacy I longed for — but could never have within the Catholic institution.

I had to face the fact that I had had trouble with parish ministry from the beginning. My spirit and my body regularly tried to tell me I would not be able to find acceptance, a sense of belonging, fulfillment, nor even an honest relationship with God as a gay male in a Catholic institution, let alone as a gay parish priest. I developed health problems regularly, usually at the same time I was having a conflict with the church hierarchy.

I asked for a year off in 1990, ten years after the crisis in Brandon, when I had had my first break from parish ministry, taking refuge in a basement room in a big house in the Wolseley area of Winnipeg.

Coming to Terms

*g*n November, 1990, at a Catholic Clergy Study Days event, a psychologist presented the four levels of burnout, Level 4 requiring chemical intervention. I was at the end of Level 3 and heading for Level 4. I discussed it with the bishop, who said he would get back to me. When we met again, he asked, "Ray, how would you feel about seeing a psychiatrist."

I think it was spiritual intervention that immediately inspired me to ask, "Bishop, will you be willing to go along with whatever the psychiatrist suggests?"

He agreed that he would, and in early 1991 the psychiatrist, Dr. Zywina, recommended I take the year off as I had wanted. The bishop, in turn, asked that I agree to see the psychiatrist on a regular basis.

But I was not yet quite through with parish ministry. I wasn't long back in Winnipeg after leaving Dunrea when I was asked to take on an interim placement at an ethnic parish in the city. As I walked into my first Sunday service in that church, a large statue of Mary stood at the entrance, flanked by candles on both sides and in front. The plaster mould of her toes had been worn almost completely away from having been touched and fondled so much. Almost every candle was lit, the small ones, at twenty-five cents each, and the larger ones at a dollar each.

As I began the service, some parishioners stayed at the statue praying rather than participate with the congregation. As soon as the mass ended and the final hymn was beginning, many headed for the exits, others went to pray at the various statues, others started mingling and talking. I found the entire experience unsettling. Though they were kind, generous and thoughtful people, and I did feel their sincere intentions, I was not used to such religiosity. There was nothing spiritual about the rituals, nor the Sunday services; they were mere duties to be performed. With that experience, my nagging discomfort and confusion around parish ministry was revived.

At our first meeting, Dr. Zywina asked me to go to the Rehfit Centre in Winnipeg where I was wired up and put through a series of stress tests. The following day, I was told to rest for the next few weeks because my blood pressure was so dangerously high I was in danger of having a fatal heart attack —- the result of forcing myself to stay extremely busy and not taking care of myself. Following his orders, my body and mind were forced to stop running in all directions. My body was giving me an ultimatum! *"Stop, or I will shut-down!"* Though I felt fine, the warning had to be taken seriously.

Two weeks later, after starting an exercise program at the Reh-fit Centre, I returned to see Dr. Zywina. He began by saying, "Ray, you have to learn how to be good to yourself."

"I don't know what you mean," I replied, holding back tears.

"I know you don't," he said.

I knew what the words meant, but didn't know how they applied to me, yet I knew they probably did. I had an excuse for everything he suggested.

Go for walks? "To where?"

Find a hobby? "Don't have time."

Develop relationships? "I deal with people all day." Read? "I read a lot of articles and pastoral books." Then he asked me to treat myself to a movie, a meal, a concert.

At forty-one, I had come to a critical point in my life and would have to face many issues. The tears would not be held back. To better get in touch with my feelings, I was asked to join support groups in which my feelings could be shared and explored, and to continue seeing him every two weeks. I was not an addict but I attended weekly meetings of alcoholics anonymous, sexaholics anonymous, and co-dependency anonymous. I also joined the Manitoba Men's Network. Men were divided into random groups of about eight and met regularly to share whatever they wanted to share about their lives and their feelings. I remained with the same group for several years. I also joined the Winnipeg Art Gallery and went to weekly Tai Chi lessons.

The support groups used the language of helplessness, powerlessness, impulsiveness, manipulation, perfectionism and control, all of which I could relate to. I had not "come out" as a gay male even to myself, let alone to any group but, through all of it, I finally began to understand and confront my own sexual orientation, but I kept it secret.

I also joined an alternative healing group, which was a very eclectic group; we met monthly, stressing holistic health, using various professional groups, cultures, ideologies, religions and sects. A day workshop on holistic health helped me put a structure to, and gain further clarification around my shrink's comment that I needed to learn how to be good to myself

The "spiritual" language of "being present" to myself and to others that I learned struck me profoundly, and subsequently became an important element in the clinical training that I would subsequently begin in 1995.

Over the course of a few weeks, my interest was aroused and I went to a bookstore and chose a book that caught my attention on the topic of narcissism, *The Drama of the Gifted Child,* by Alice Miller. Then I wanted to go somewhere to reflect and asked to spend November and December at the Trappist Monastery north of Toronto. Once again, I found myself living with monks as I had in the summer of 1967. This time they were busy making Christmas fruit cakes and, just like at the previous monastery, I worked in the bakery.

Those two months proved very difficult for me. That monastery, which has since closed, was in the middle of 350 acres of beautiful rolling hills with great walking paths, tall pine trees, and lots of deer. When it snowed, the landscape became overwhelmingly beautiful. In that winter paradise, nature allowed me my first opportunity to scream at the top of my lungs over what I felt were my many losses.

"It is not so much for its beauty that the forest makes a claim upon men's hearts, as for that subtle something, that quality of air, that emanation from old trees, that so wonderfully changes and renews a weary spirit."
— Robert Louis Stevenson

Miller's book, *The Drama of the Gifted Child,* was shocking and surprising... as if the author knew me personally and perhaps had lived as an invisible person at my side during every moment of my childhood. I didn't know what to make of that. Every sentence, evaluation and observation made it seem as if she also knew my mother intimately. But before the book, I had never thought of my mother in that particular way, nor had I ever heard someone speak about me in the same way, but as I read, I knew it all to be true.

Reading *The Drama of the Gifted Child* was like watching a movie about my own childhood. At the end of each section, I had to go into the woods to cry and scream. Sometimes I felt I would lose my breath completely and drop where I stood. I felt vulnerable, exposed, and yet not alone. I felt the presence of God in the woods, accepting me, allowing me to cry and scream, day after day, week after week.

Sometimes I returned exhausted, yet grateful for the silence of my room and an opportunity to sleep early. God had given me the time to read, to cry and to pray, and with no one expecting anything from me. Several times a day, I would do just that, cry my thanks to God for that sacred time and place.

Alice Miller writes that, "If both spiritual hunger and dependency on human loving are denied or rejected, the only thing left is narcissism." At first those words haunted me, and then they became part of my spiritual journey.

Miller's book brought me to the realization that I had been an emotionally abused child. I came to accept that my parents never intended to "emotionally abuse" me, but they had. They did the best they could with what they had and knew, and had the best intentions at heart. I perceived my childhood much differently as a child than I did after reading *The Drama of the Gifted Child*.

As I came to understand my spiritual journey, I accepted the grace that my parents had been for me because without them, and my experiences, this book would not have been possible.

From the very beginning, I had no choice but to comply totally with the needs and feelings of my mother and to ignore my own. I had never questioned my version of the happy childhood I supposedly had enjoyed but, with hindsight, the more I learned to follow my impulses, to express my own thoughts, to believe in what I believed in, and not in what I had been taught and told to believe in, the weaker became my allegiance to the Catholic institution, and the more compassionate and understanding I became towards my mother. Unfortunately, the opportunity for my mother and me to speak about it was never possible.

My mother had said to me, as we stood before her own mother lying in a casket, "I don't know why I can't cry." But I knew why she couldn't cry. She had been raised as I had been raised. She was looking at the woman in that casket who had taken her childhood from her, who had used her daughter to get respect, just as I was standing beside the woman who had similarly used me.

Growing up, I had never experienced natural contact with my own emotions and wishes, which would have given me strength and self-esteem. I needed to have lived out my feelings, to be sad, despairing, or in need of help, without the fear of making my mother insecure. But that had never been possible.

I needed to have allowed myself to be afraid when threatened or angry when my wishes were not fulfilled. I needed to know not only what I didn't want, but also what I did want, and be able to express those desires irrespective of whether I would be loved or hated by my mother for doing so. But that had never been possible.

Finally realizing these things — my losses — I went for my walks far into the woods where, with no one around, I screamed and screamed till near exhaustion. The woods enabled me to expose myself to emotions that had welled up out of my earliest childhood and to experience the helplessness and ambivalence of that period. Clinging tendencies and feelings of helplessness mingled with long damned-up rage against my mother, who had not been available to me. The monastic environment allowed me to finally experience the pain, and to give up the old illusion of a happy childhood.

And through it all, I guess I grew up. I discovered a new need, a need to live according to my "true self" and to no longer allow myself to be forced to earn love.

The monks always got together on Christmas Eve, after evening prayers, for a special celebration. In the privacy of their monastery a tree was decorated, tables covered with wines, cheeses and goodies. Everyone was able to speak freely with one another. In that rarefied atmosphere of seasonal joy, I took the opportunity to thank them for their hospitality.

Because they were not used to such socializing, the evening ended gradually, and late. The following morning, a beautiful Christmas mass was held. The Christmas tree remained lit and the rest of the day was kept in silence and simplicity, in sharp contrast to the following day, Boxing Day, in downtown Toronto.

Before leaving the monastery, I cherished one last walk in the woods. I felt a deep peace knowing my mother would no longer have emotional and psychological control over me. And I felt a deep sadness knowing that at the same time, she would never understand my independence and never be able to accept my behaviours, my thinking, my feelings, my emotions, and my desires.

I felt a deep gratitude to God for having given me the opportunity that allowed me to experience a rebirth in my own life, a gift that I will always cherish.

Upon my return to Winnipeg in January, 1992, I embarked on what I hoped would be a better experience of parish ministry. The Oblate Fathers had ministered among the aboriginal and Inuit people in our diocese for many years, but with recruitment declining, the need for our diocesan priests to serve these communities increased. With few diocesan priests culturally prepared to serve aboriginal communities, my request to the bishop to take studies in native spirituality at the University of British Columbia and to minister among the aboriginal people in our diocese was welcomed. Remembering how much

I had enjoyed the simplicity of the religious and spiritual lives of the Inuit, I was very pleased as well.

June and July of 1992 were spent studying with aboriginal people from all over the world and learning a great deal from them as they shared their rituals, spiritual beliefs, customs and tribal links. There was a spirit of tolerance and respect among us for their belief in the power of dreams, visions, rituals, fasting, and the "little people". Upon my return, I was asked to be the administrator of five communities located two hours north of Winnipeg, one of which was aboriginal — the Lake Manitoba Reserve. I felt very comfortable with the aboriginal people, but as I was leaving the reserve one evening during a heavy rain, which made the road very muddy and slippery, I suddenly felt a strong need to pull over to the side of the road. The car came to a stop and I began to cry uncontrollably.

"Thank you God for bringing me home," I kept saying. But that northern reserve was not my home.

After some time, I managed to pull myself together and go home, but I was on the road again the next evening on my way to a powwow. When I arrived, I found only an elder sitting by a large fire that was encircled by benches waiting for the absent crowds.

"Where is everyone?" I asked.

"It was cancelled because we thought it would start to rain again," the elder said, then asked me, "Did you see what was in the sky when you arrived?"

"No," I responded.

"A double rainbow... I think the reason I was called to stay seated here was to meet you," he said.

We sat quietly for a few minutes, then I asked him if I could tell him about what had happened to me the previous evening. He was okay with that, so I did. Afterwards, he said, "You have probably been among our people in a previous life and your spirit is now back among its people."

Somehow, that made sense to me; I had always felt comfortable among aboriginal people.

"You are being called to be a warrior of the rainbow," the elder added.

At the time, I didn't understand what that meant and we didn't talk a lot more, preferring to sit quietly and enjoy the fire before we left.

Most people in that aboriginal community were not preoccupied with church regulations. The dominant preoccupation was with problems of addictions and domestic abuse, which were rampant. Families were divided for many reasons: because of separate ties to other denominations, political and legal struggles within the community, and young people being attracted to lifestyles depicted in television advertising. Many had also struggled with the effects that the Canadian residential school system had had on them.

Some were grateful for the education and support they had received in that system because they needed it to enter southern society. But for others, the residential system had been abusive, inflicting humiliation and pain on them, in part, through being told their aboriginal beliefs and practices were not of God and that they would have to forsake their aboriginal language, culture, customs, traditions and spirituality if they wanted to be pleasing to

God. As a gay priest with the burden of his own secret, I could relate to their struggle.

Many aboriginal parents had been left with feelings of shame, resentment, guilt and the hope that their children would be able to "get done" in a church, as they had been as children. Many were burdened by the resurgence of their own spirituality and rituals, which were no longer considered illegal and which were calling them to their root experiences of a relationship with God. Families were torn once again between wanting to experience what they had been taught was pagan, and the fear of rejection by some self-righteous family members who had come to believe the old ways were, indeed, truly not of God.

My parents had offered their children a Catholic faith foundation that they had hoped we would also cherish. I could understand those parents who found it very painful to see their children making different choices in the practice of their faith. Parents and guardians would ask themselves where they had gone wrong, and if God would judge them for the choices their children were making. Would God forgive their children and continue to bless them; would He one day allow their children to be with Him in Heaven?

We had imposed our faith on them as a "gift" and now we were making them feel guilty for not continuing to go along with what we had been asking of them and they, in turn, had seen us as punishing their children by not letting them receive the rites of passage. I was once again getting very tired of this kind of church unreasonable heavy handedness, not to mention all the same old issues with parish ministry, which persisted. I was determined to keep my sanity this time and, although I very much related to the aboriginal people, I decided to move on. However, I was determined to right what I saw as a major wrong before I left.

When it came time for me to leave the area, I let it be known that the Sunday before my departure I would baptize the children who had not yet been baptized, knowing that this would probably be their only chance to "get done". I asked that a family member attend three meetings to instruct and prepare them, and that the family member agree to share the information with anyone wanting to be baptized. Godparents and sponsors had to be chosen, copies of birth certificates were needed, a white stole had to be made for each person being baptized, and the families needed to organize a reception in the hall after the service.

For my part, I needed to organize the service, prepare someone to write up the certificates, and ask singers and musicians from the aboriginal parish in Winnipeg to help us out. The instructions were well received and the people were excited as everyone prepared for the big day. But I had seen people's plans change quickly on the reserve so one question played on my mind throughout all the preparations — how many would actually show up?

Thankfully, the weather on the big day turned out to be beautiful because it was, indeed, a busy day. The church and reception hall were ready and the ladies had completed preparations. The singers were in place and practicing before the service. I had everything set up and ready to go. Then it started... car after car arrived. Within minutes children were everywhere and everyone was dressed in their best attire. The babies, some of the children, and a few adults who were to be baptized, stood out from the crowd with their white stoles around their necks; dozens and dozens of white stoles dotted the congregation. Literally hundreds of people gathered... and I felt a bit like John the Baptiser.

The service was organized chaos. Everyone seemed so happy and excited. I could tell they knew exactly what was happening as they responded to questions and instructions. With so many people, it took a few hours before we got to the reception, which consisted of an abundance of aboriginal cuisine. The singers came to the hall to offer entertainment, as did almost every child on the reserve. The adults, especially the elders, were very grateful. It was a service I will never forget.

Many aboriginal people knew how the Catholic Church felt about many of their beliefs and practices but rather than argue with the hierarchy, they kept their culture and beliefs close to their hearts, which was their way of being in a spiritual relationship with God, whom they called Manitou.

I have always felt for people trying to "fit in" because I have never been able to do so. I have always identified with people who have a unique relationship with God because I believe that's what I always had. And I have always felt for people who have been made to feel guilty for how they live because I, with my fantasies and knowing the church would disapprove, have always felt guilty about my secret.

Aboriginal issues played a significant part in my spiritual journey, and through the experiences I had among them I redefined my relationship with God — now a relationship outside the institution of the church.

As a priest, I was regularly presented with a steady stream of documents from the Vatican covering almost every imaginable aspect of life. In late 1989, for example, the Pope's head of the Congregation for the Doctrine of the Faith, his "guardian of orthodoxy" (currently the Pope), issued a document warning Roman Catholics that Zen, yoga, and transcendental meditation could "degenerate into a cult of the body." It was followed by a day-long workshop for all the priests in the diocese.

The priest conducting the workshop had been presented as an "expert" on the topic of cults and the New Age Movement. I remember being more afraid of him than anything he had to say. His job was to convince us priests of the dangers, so we, in turn, could enlighten our parishioners.

Then, in late 1992, the institution released its "New Catechism", the first since the Council of Trent in 1566. It was hailed by Pope John Paul II as one of the major events in the recent history of the Roman Catholic Church. Included were birth control as a matter of self-discipline; infertile periods as acceptable; ordination limited to baptized men, in keeping with Christ's own example; and the ordination of women as impossible. Homosexuality went against natural law, while homosexuals were to be treated with compassion and fairness and urged to be chaste.

Without knowing the story, on May 5, 1995, I saw the movie *The Priest*.. It was about a gay priest who was caught by the police in a sexual encounter. His bishop and parishioners reacted badly. I sat stunned and numb, watching what seemed to be my own life on film — other viewers left the theatre in anger and disgust.

"*I must not be alone,*" *I* thought to myself, wondering if the movie had been based on a real person. Leaving the theatre, I once again felt the loneliness of having had no one to share the experience with and was filled with the fear of realizing that if my bishop ever found out about me I would probably be treated the same way as the poor fellow in the movie.

That film had an overwhelming impact on me. I felt great fear, but also encouragement because I felt more confident that I was not the only one with the secret.

In July of 1995, a priest named Father Henry suggested I have a talk with the Catholic chaplain at the prison in Headingley, just outside Winnipeg.

"Why do you want me to see him?" I asked. "I don't know him."

"Just ask to see him," he said, so, a few days later, I met the chaplain and he asked why I had come.

"Father Henry asked me to see you, but I don't know why."

"Ray, tell me your story," he said.

He patiently listened to me, then said, "Sounds similar to my own story," and asked, "Have you ever considered being a chaplain?"

"As a parish priest, I had never seen it as an option," I replied.

He then sent out a fax and shortly afterwards received a response, which he handed to me and asked me to give to the bishop. It asked that I be allowed to take clinical training to become a chaplain.

"The bishop will not agree," I said emphatically. "The last thing he said to me was, 'The next time you come here, it will be on my terms, not yours'."

The chaplain asked me to swallow my pride and make an appointment to see the bishop anyway. I did as he suggested.

"Do not be afraid to go out on a limb ... That's where the fruit is."
— Anonymous

As I walked into the chancery, the only thing missing was a red carpet. I was greeted like the prodigal son returning from a life of debauchery and squandering — the squandering part did not apply to me.

Everyone greeted and welcomed me back. After a fraternal hug from the bishop and an offer of a cup of coffee, I was welcomed into his office. He seemed genuinely pleased to see me again.

After about a fifteen-minute update, I showed him the note that had been given to me by the prison chaplain. His expression changed dramatically. He put the paper on his desk and stood with his right hand outstretched towards me and his index finger pointing directly between my eyes.

"You get the f— out of here," he screamed at the top of his lungs. I stood frozen for a moment, then he continued. "Come back in three days and I'll tell you where you're going."

Humiliated and stunned, I left his office under the glare of the others present, who looked at me in silence and dismay.

I went to sleep early that night, still stunned, tired and confused. The following morning at about 8 a.m., the phone rang; it was the bishop, and my heart leapt to my throat.

Sounding very distraught, he said, "Ray, could you please come to the office as soon as possible... today."

Half an hour later, I arrived and was offered another cup of coffee and wondered if I would have time to finish it before he threw me out again. He was visibly shaken and had difficulty speaking.

"I had a dream last night," he began. Pacing back and forth in front of his desk, he continued. "In my dream, I spent the entire night in hell."

This was not the time to offer my opinion, though I was sorely tempted.

"I had been sent there because I had refused to help a brother priest," he said.

That dream must have been as clear to him as Joseph's had been in the scriptures when he was asked to flee to Egypt.

Then, as he slowly sat down, he apologized, signed the note that had been given by the chaplain, and added, "I'll be phoning the co-ordinator of chaplains to ask him to help you in any way he can, and the diocese will pay for your studies."

I had made it; my coffee was down to the last drop and I was still there. But, with a thank-you and a handshake, I was once again on my way out, and once again, to the surprise of the mesmerized staff, I was leaving as stunned as I had been the day before. But inside I felt much better and phoned the chaplain to give him the news as soon as I got home.

When I later recounted the incident to my new bishop in 2002, his response was, "Well, it makes for a good story,"

"*Whatever!*" I thought to myself, and prepared to begin my new studies.

4

Approaching Wholeness

Chaplaincy

*D*uring my clinical pastoral education studies, I didn't have to deal with the parish politics that emanated from the tensions between the demands of the hierarchy and the ritual needs of parishioners. Most importantly, I was free of the helpless frustration of being in the middle, trying to be at the service of both groups.

I was about to study the writings of Henri J. M. Nouwen, who had died in 1996 while vacationing in Holland where he was born in 1932. A priest and professor at Yale and Harvard, Nouwen was also the man I had met at the Trappist monastery in 1967 and was later described to me as one of the best known and most honoured spiritual writers of our time.

Through dozens of books, such as *Reaching Out* and *The Wounded Healer,* Nouwen invited countless people to enter the spiritual life more deeply_ Some of his important endeavours had been in early support of the civil rights movement, his engagement in the cause of peace, and work with disabled members of the L'Arche community.

He had always been immersed in the social, as well as the spiritual, dimensions of the gospel.

In 1985, Nouwen wrote that women had a real call to ministry and that homosexuals had a unique vocation in the Christian community. After he died, we began hearing about his sexual orientation. I'm sure he was only too aware of the scandal that his private life would have created and how he would have been treated had that fact been revealed while he was alive.

The first basic unit of my clinical studies took place at Headingley Correctional Centre just west of Winnipeg; the second, and my first advanced units, were at the Health Sciences Centre in Winnipeg. Issues addressed included one's role as a chaplain, one's identity, and the meaning of professional presence and due process. I had to learn what it meant to "be present" to someone and not to escape as soon as I felt rejected or intimidated, or as soon as I was finished with "my business". I had to learn to sit with someone without expectations or agenda.

When those studies were completed, my supervisor from the hospital gave me the following evaluation:

> *"Theologically, Ray is well-grounded and solidly identified. He is a compassionate and pastoral Roman Catholic Priest who loves and respects his church, but suffers from what he experiences to be its rigid institutional structures. He claims his autonomy and authority by offering a non judgmental and compassionate ministry to those individuals and groups who are in need of this comfort. His theological*

> *perspectives were the broadest within the peer group and he has modelled this kind of openness for his peers as well as for our department. At the same time, he values and generously offers the healing sacraments of his religious tradition when they are requested I affirm Ray's theological and pastoral stance as I believe they converge well with the demands of the ministry of chaplaincy."*

Chaplaincy clients often wanted spiritual comfort, not just religious rituals. That was refreshing and exciting for me, yet unsettling. A transition was taking place within me that I didn't fully understand. I had thought that words such as faith, religion and spirituality were terms for one and the same reality.

As a Catholic, I had been influenced and directed into various forms of spirituality through the works of a number of Catholic writers: St. Francis, St. Theresa, St. Augustine, St. John of the Cross, St. Bernard, St. Benedict, and St. Ignatius, to name a few. These men and women had written at times in history when the Catholic Church had ultimate control and power, and within a culture that saw virtue and sainthood in practicing complete obedience. For me, the "language" was of submission, guilt, obedience, and self-denial.

Since childhood, my "spiritual hunger" for answers to the many questions I had about beliefs and doctrines made me feel I was just difficult, contrary, and somehow unfaithful. I had no difficulty believing in God, but I had trouble with the notion that I had to believe all the doctrines for the sake of my soul.

In both the hospital and corrections, however, I spoke with clients who had very different spiritual views from those I had been raised with, and from those of former Catholic parishioners. Within chaplaincy training group dynamics, I was able to share my own views without judgment, suspicion, ridicule or scandal, and began to realize that my spirituality looked beyond organized religion. In my thirst to satisfy my spiritual hunger at the time, while still accepting my Roman Catholic faith, it was refreshing to be able to question and articulate my own views, and to receive the feedback and support of others.

Nothing remained a greater human mystery, nor a more popular topic of daily discussion at the Health Sciences Centre than death. We all know we are going to die and there is nothing we can do to prevent it. The only questions are when, and whether death marks the termination of our existence. There is much bewilderment about the reality of death and what, if anything, lies beyond it.

My hospital experience showed me that life can exceed our desire for it. Consequently, an increasingly important question for many is the question of how people can die with dignity, including the right to die when they would choose to.

Perhaps surprisingly to some at the time, something else that helped us understand the meaning of life was the New Age Movement. It was often spoken about, along with other "fringe" activities, such as meditation, astrology, tarot cards, reincarnation, out-of-body experiences, and dream analysis. The New Age Movement had become a significant spiritual movement. It focused on the tapping of one's potential, personal spirituality, the spirit world, the oneness of creation, the limitless potential of humanity, the possibility of transforming the self, and today's world, into something better.

In my desire to move beyond religiosity to spirituality, I read O'Murchu's book, *Reclaiming Spirituality*. It gave me the language I needed to articulate my spiritual experience, and helped me understand that a new era was upon us, an era in which many would no longer accept being controlled by guilt and shame and intimidation.

As one of my term positions while studying at the hospital, I was assigned to the intensive care unit and asked to develop an in-service for the staff on spirituality and wellness. The outline I developed stated that God calls us "to be" healthy, and that we are "healthy" when we are in harmony within ourselves — within the relationship between body, mind and spirit. We are "in health" when there is harmony in our relationship with our higher power. The prophet Jesus said the same thing 2,000 years ago when he referred to "loving God with all our being, and our neighbour as ourselves."

After completing the course in clinical pastoral education, I was hired by Corrections Manitoba as a staff chaplain at Headingley. For the first time in my priesthood, I was free from parish routine and was able to be more open about God and who I really was. In my previous religious life, I had felt stifled by the church. Ironically, I had to land in a prison to feel free.

My work involved counselling inmates who were dealing with a number of different issues and crises. Though the work was difficult, I found it rewarding, personally challenging, and spiritually fulfilling.

Chaplaincy serves the spiritual needs of individuals in a wide variety of institutions: hospitals, universities, the military and prisons. Although endorsed by a particular faith community, chaplains serve the institution that employs them, not just their respective churches. As a chaplain, I had a foot in two worlds; I was a government employee with my own salary, living independently from the diocese, but still a priest. I was living a celibate life in a secular world — but was I?

I had been a closeted gay priest for twenty-five years, careful to keep my secret, to separate my various lives. But living one step removed from the church in my own apartment, away from the fishbowl of parish life, I began to live more openly. I felt a tremendous sense of independence from the bishop, from church activities, and from parishioners' expectations. After all, prison inmates accepted me as I was.

I felt free to go to gay bars, to meet other men for sexual encounters, and to make a life for myself as part of the gay community. I joined LAMBDA, attended a gay spiritual support group, and went to Gay Pride events. But I was naïve to think I could live such a lifestyle and be a priest at the same time without the two worlds eventually colliding.

I felt I had been called to the priesthood, and had found a way of living out my priesthood as a chaplain, but my new-found "out" life was just as important to me as my priesthood. I began to think of my new life as an expansion of my secret with God. However, secrets have a way of not staying secret.

Coming Out

*A*cknowledging that I was gay to some friends included socializing in the gay community, joining gay social activities, gay spirituality discussion groups, and attending gay lectures and discussions on "coming out" and the gay lifestyle. Being a chaplain and a Roman Catholic priest, I was putting myself at risk of exposure, intimidation and public scandal.

Shortly after moving into my apartment, I received a call from a former acquaintance.

"Hi Father Ray, this is James."

James, who had moved to Vancouver some years previous, was the son of Clarisse, a woman who had been very helpful to me in Dunrea.

"Don and I are going to Dunrea to visit Mom and wondered if we could visit you in Winnipeg on the way?" he asked. Don was James's equally good looking partner.

"Sure James," I answered with excitement. "Will you be in Winnipeg for a few days?" I asked, with hope in my voice.

"Would you have room for us?"

"Sure, I have a fold-out futon in the living room," I said.

"Great! We'll call you in a few days, Father Ray."

Our first evening together happened to be a Friday and they told me about their plans.

"We want to go to a gay bar and we would like you to come with us," James said.

I hadn't "come out" to James and Don but James later confessed that his "gaydar" had figured me out not long after I had first met him back in Dunrea and had spent time being supportive of him, which he had appreciated. They were content to wait for me to finally come out to them, which I did. The revelation had them gleaming with the self satisfaction of knowing their gaydar had been accurate.

That Friday evening however, I said, "No...I'm sure you two will have a great time...I'll give you my spare key."

But they wouldn't take no for an answer. After wasting some time trying to reason with them, I succumbed and went along. As we entered the bar, I was almost immediately approached by a husky, muscular stud, who later became one of my "regular" visitors.

"Ray" (which I insisted on being called while we were together), "you don't waste much time, do you?" James was quick to observe.

After the weekend with James and Don, I decided to call Suzette and come out to her as well. She was the daughter of one of the families I had befriended in Brandon and was living in Winnipeg at the time and had come out to me. I desperately needed someone to share with and I knew I could trust her. Afterwards, we hugged and cried and became close friends, indulging in regular coffee and chocolate cookie encounters.

Suzette has always been a very attractive woman, able to turn the head of every male who crosses her path. When we were together and would notice that going on, she would smile at me and say, "Ray, he's all yours." Our conversations would have shocked our parents, embarrassed some of our friends, and aroused other gays.

Through gay chat lines, my encounters were mostly "one- night stands", though some became friends and others became "regulars". Going to socials, the bars and bath houses became lucrative in terms of gay contact, but none of the encounters developed into relationships because, as a priest, I couldn't chance being in a long-term relationship, though I never admitted that to any of the men who expressed a long-term interest. Of those I did tell about my being a priest, some were shocked into flight while others felt even more comfortable with me.

In time, that unavailability — my inability to make a commitment with anyone — caused intense loneliness, even in the midst of all my one-night stands and regulars. I always knew that at the end of the day, even if someone stayed over for the night, he would not be there to comfort and support me and would never be able to be my "significant other", which was what my soul had always pained for. Henri Nouwen would have known and understood the pain of my experience.

In May, 1997, I was hired full-time in prison chaplaincy. My priesthood protected my sexual orientation in that anyone with suspicions about me wouldn't say anything to me about them. Many, especially Catholics, thought priests had a special supernatural grace to suppress their human feelings and needs while others thought of priests as eunuchs, or at least asexual. But those who knew differently spoke behind my back and among themselves. Being exposed as a gay male in a male prison by some guard or an inmate's gaydar could have been difficult, and dangerous because of homophobia.

Because sexual contacts in prison were always discrete and often engaged in in order to have human needs met, they were not necessarily an indication of sexual orientation. When someone spoke about their sexual orientation, my calm acceptance was supportive and affirming for them. On a number of occasions, an inmate would say, "You seem to understand me," and I would think, *If you only knew.*

It was during this time that I met Chris, a one-night stand. He asked that we remain friends. We began meeting every few weeks and he became a valuable and knowledgeable mentor within the gay community. As a gay political activist, he was very aware of the "gay scene" in the community.

After a few months, when he said he appreciated our friendship, I began to feel very guilty because I had not told him I was a priest out of fear of possible rejection and of scandalizing him, which actually would have been laughable.

"Chris, I have something I want to say to you that is very difficult for me," I nervously managed one day.

"We'll talk about it the next time we meet," he replied bluntly.

Two weeks later, as he made himself comfortable on the couch with a Corona in hand, he asked, "Well, what did you want to tell me that was going to be so difficult to say?"

I thought I was going to pass out but there was no backing away.

"I'm a priest!" I blurted out.

"That's it, that's the secret you found so hard to tell me... aren't all priests gay?"

After a few hours of painful disclosure, he asked. "Promise me that you won't do your priest thing at my funeral, should I die before you?"

"I promise."

When there's a hole in a dike and then it finally breaks, it's difficult to hold the water back. A fellow priest, to whom I had come out, told me about a convocation of gay priests that he wanted to attend in the United States. I asked for more details and, without telling anyone, made plans to attend. Because of the "Flood of the Century" in 1997 in Winnipeg, our formal church retreat was cancelled and we were asked to make our own arrangements. I asked the bishop for permission to attend a retreat in the States and, since I was not asking for financial assistance and was going during my holiday time, he gave his permission and no further questions were asked.

When we arrived, as I walked into a room of a few hundred gay priests, tears came to my eyes.

"Are you alright?" someone asked.

"Have you any idea how I feel right now?" I sobbed. "Until recently, I had thought I was the only gay priest in the world."

"We have all felt that way at one time," he replied.

The weekend was electrifying; the liturgies, the speakers, the sharing, the sexual energy — it was all so overwhelming. The retreat helped me to know, accept and celebrate who I was. I had always known that I was different.

In 1999, I attended gay pride celebrations in Toronto, Vancouver and Montreal, but in Winnipeg, I often felt judged and unaccepted, which made my "coming out" process even more difficult. To many in the gay community who felt like outsiders in the church, I personified the institution. Some saw me as living in two different worlds. And I feared scandalizing those who recognized me as much as I feared being rejected or outed to the hierarchy.

At bars and other social events, I just wanted to be among like-minded people but often felt like an outsider to the faith community, like a leper.

My father died that same year. My siblings didn't know what to say nor what to expect from each other. We had become strangers to one another.

Dad had had a strong devotion to the Mother of Jesus so I asked the church soloist to sing "Ave Maria". It was very moving. And out of respect for me as a priest, the bishop sat near the altar throughout the service. Dad's spirit felt privileged and grateful to his son.

Mother stayed strong, as usual, keeping her feelings and thoughts to herself. My heart went out to her and I did my best to help her be comfortable and cared for. I ignored her comments and did what I felt needed to be done. Leaving was painful for me, knowing we had grown apart and feeling that I couldn't do anything about it.

On my return to Winnipeg, I offered to assist on a part-time basis at St. Ann's, an inner city parish that had just lost its priest. I enjoyed the people and looked forward to Sunday worship, which was the only time I could offer the community because of my full- time work at the prison. But, once again unable to live up to the expectations of the pillars of the parish, after only seven months there, the pastor thought it best for me to stop offering Sunday services, rather than try to address those expectations.

In late 2001, despite a busy ministry and being comfortable in the prison setting — imprisonment being familiar to me — I felt intense loneliness and emptiness and compensated by spending more time and money in the gay social life. It took a critical incident at that point to keep me from full-blown depression arising from a sense of meaninglessness.

The 'Outing' — Part 2

*"The best time to plant a tree was 20 years ago
The next best time is now."*
— Chinese Proverb

The February, 2002, edition of a newsletter for gay priests began with the words, "Happy are those who dream dreams and are willing to pay the price to make them come true." That quote set the theme for my new year.

The signs were there; something was about to happen. Silenced, a number of priests and nuns were not allowed to speak out publicly. The most painful for me to read about were Sister Jeannine Gramick and Father Robert Nugent, who had worked for decades in ministry with gay and lesbian Catholics. In silencing them and no longer allowing them to minister to homosexual people, in the view of many, the Vatican had exercised blatant discrimination. The church kept using "scandal" as a reason for its persecution of theologians, and others, yet more were scandalized by the actions of the church than by those causing the so-called scandals.

Despite the fact that Nugent had spoken on "silent witness" and Gramick had used official church documents in support of the right of church members to speak their opinions and to form their consciences, their arguments were refuted and they were silenced. It came as a great disappointment, but certainly no surprise to me, that this would be the inevitable consequence for anyone who confronted a homophobic church.

My Sunday evening arrival at the Toronto airport on my way to Southdown was in sharp contrast to my Friday morning arrival at work at Headingley Correctional Centre. The Southdown chauffeur was no ordinary chauffeur. He was used to spotting people like me exiting the airport — apprehensive individuals looking for a white limo.

"Are you Father Ray?" he asked, standing by his car at the curb.

"Yes I am," I said.

"Welcome to Toronto," he replied. "Let me help you with your bags."

As he opened the back door of the car for me to enter, I thought of Julia Roberts in the movie *Pretty Women* sitting in the back seat of a luxurious limo.

The driver knew his passenger was uncomfortable, fearful, embarrassed. I had been given an ultimatum and he knew it. He had met many others like me and was experienced and well trained in how to make me feel at ease.

We arrived after an hour of pleasantry while driving through the beautiful rolling farm lands north of Toronto. He talked about all the men and women he had made the same trip with and who had been so grateful for the experience I was about to have. One thing he was right about for certain was his description of the centre and its setting; they were both beautiful.

A matron came out to greet me and, after thanking the driver, I followed her inside. I felt as if I had left part of myself at the airport and was now on autopilot, leaving the control of events to others in what appeared to be a five-star resort.

I was immediately struck by how the other "guests" I encountered looked controlled, lacking warmth and conversation, as if they were from another world. After a coffee and an uncomfortable chitchat, I was led to my room and asked to complete a questionnaire that sat next to a schedule on the desk. Obviously, life at Southdown was going to be quite regimented: breakfast at 8 a.m., which I could find by asking anyone I met; followed by my first appointment at 9 a.m. An entire week of appointments had been set up, with at least three different shrinks a day and a daily interview with my assigned "main" doctor.

I filled out the questionnaire, which asked for detailed information about my childhood, adolescence, parents, family members, education, parish experiences, friends, etc, etc. Two hours later and very tired, I made for the bed, remembering to set my alarm.

At 7 a.m. I opened my blinds to a beautiful landscape of rolling hills, a manicured property, a pond, lawn chairs and park benches at various meditation points. I quickly got ready and said good morning to the first person I met.

"Where's the cafeteria?" I dutifully asked.

"Follow me," he said blandly.

The people at Southdown certainly knew how to treat men and women who were used to a privileged lifestyle, or perhaps thought they deserved it. There was no mistaking this was a five- star establishment, chefs and all.

The round cafeteria tables each held six people comfortably. "Good morning, may I join you?" I asked a group that had room for one more.

"By all means," came a southern accent from an elderly gentleman directly across the table.

We were considered patients, and were treated like patients and it quickly became apparent that most of my companions were under heavy medication, and had been for a long time.

"They decrease the dosage as you're feeling better," a sweet woman remarked.

I knew it; I could feel it in the air. Every day, I would be sitting with different priests and nuns from all over North America "under obedience" and filled with varying degrees of guilt, fear, anger, resentment, embarrassment, gratitude, and apprehension, yet hopeful about the future; some were just grateful for time out. Many seemed reserved, distant, sad (some very sad), and others seemed right at home.

A large, quite impressive buffet was laid out for breakfast with a variety of cereals, juices, fruits, breads, eggs, bacon, ham, jams, coffees, teas, and water, with or without a wedge of lemon.

Lunch and supper were even more outstanding. We were graced with the presentation of variety, quantity and choice — five — star food - at every meal. General attentiveness was second perhaps only to that given folks in palliative care.

"Is there anything else we can get for you?"

"No, thank you."

I was not medicated during my evaluation week and could feel the energy around me — it wasn't positive. Most of the others had been through their week of evaluation, had returned to their homes to discuss the results with their superiors, and then been asked to come back to Southdown for treatment. "Treatments" could last several months to as long as a year for depression, alcoholism, sexual misconduct and other "questionable behaviours".

I knew that it was costing my diocese a $1,000 a day to keep me there. This was serious business, the best food and shrinks that money could buy.

At the beginning of that week of assessment, my primary shrink asked, "Father Ray, what are you hoping to get from Southdown?"

"I hope to understand the reasons for the crises I have been having every five years."

"I don't think we are going to be able to do that for you," he said. "But we will be able to give you tests to assess intellectual, pathological, psychological and health issues, and to make suggestions to you and to your bishop."

I immediately began losing hope that something positive would come out of the experience.

The evaluation I was given at the end of the week stated that I had a sexual addiction because I refused to give up my active gay lifestyle; I had told my shrink that he and his colleagues were ignorant of the normal psychology of a gay male. My remarks had the same effect on him as water on a duck's back.

Secondly, the evaluation stated that I had a disorder referred to as a "narcissistic personality".

Thirdly, they considered me to be a liability to the church because I was not accepting celibacy, and could implicate the church in further accusations and possible lawsuits.

It was concluded that I could not be rehabilitated, nor reprogrammed, as I had interpreted it, back into a celibate, clerical box so that I would not cause any more waves, which was also my interpretation.

That evening, as I walked in the woods along the property, I prayed, "Dear God, speak to me through my bishop," which he wasted no time in doing.

Even after returning from Southdown, I could not recognize the signs that the priesthood was not a healthy lifestyle for me as a gay male. I was still prepared to go along with anything the bishop asked of me in order to protect myself, safeguard my own security, and to get him off my back. But the bishop had already made up his mind. With the assessment and support from Southdown stating that rehabilitation was unlikely, I had to be cut loose.

Within ten minutes of calling me into his office, the bishop said, "Ray, we have come to a crossroads. Since

Southdown says you cannot be 'rehabilitated', I am removing your faculties (my authorization to function as a priest)."

He also suggested that I request "laicization" (Ask the Pope to revoke my clerical status), which would also remove any legal ties with the diocese.

"I am no longer going to support you as a chaplain," he added. "You will need to find employment elsewhere."

Then, in a gesture of fraternal and collegial affection, he gave me a hug, which felt like it was a whole minute long, and reminded me of a certain Judas incident. Then I was asked to leave. I will never forget the feeling that came over me as I walked out — a sense of freedom   though I didn't understand why at the time.

The following day, I met with JR, the superintendent at Headingley and told him what had happened and about the assessment.

"My 'faculties' have been removed," I said.

"Oh... does that mean you are now brain dead?" he asked with a smirk.

After a needed laugh, he assured me of his support and told me I was appreciated in the institution and that a two-year term position had just come up, which I qualified for and which would give me the time to make my transition. Not only was God guiding and protecting me, he was using a prison to keep me safe.

The bishop quickly removed my benefits and privileges and offered me $25,000 to help me with my transition, and for the 24 years I had given to the diocese. His assistant had mentioned on a few occasions that the diocese wanted to offer me the money as a matter of justice.

Shortly afterwards, I went on a weekend workshop given by O'Murchu on the topic of his book *Reclaiming Spirituality*. The term "the disfunctionate church" was used but I never felt comfortable with it because it painted everyone in the church with the same brush. O'Murehu said the church hierarchy consisted of only about one percent of the whole church while the faithful, the laity, made up the remaining ninety-nine percent.

That insight prepared me for my next workshop, in June, 2002, which was on domestic abuse. I attended, along with a few correctional officers from the Domestic Abuse Unit at Headingley. As I listened, I could relate a lot of what was said to the relationship I had had with my mother, and with the hierarchy of the church — that one percent who have all the power and control and who make the final decisions on all matters.

When, as a child and later as a priest, I had believed I was the problem, that I didn't fit in, that I was not good enough, I always felt like a helpless victim, filled with fear and vulnerability. I was being emotionally abused because I didn't feel free to be myself, to know and express myself. I also feared leaving the church because I thought I would lose respect, my pension, a secured retirement with benefits, and the friends I had as a priest. The losses seemed to outweigh the benefits of freedom and peace of mind.

I not only learned a great deal through those workshops but I also acquired a language that facilitated my understanding of all that I had mistakenly hoped to get at Southdown. I understood why I hadn't fit in with the institution — I was gay!

I understood why, like clockwork, I had fallen into a crisis every few years — my body was trying to tell me it couldn't take the pain of being so alone!

I understood why I felt so lonely and trapped — the church institution would never accept me as an active gay male and would never allow me to have a significant other in my life as a priest!

And I understood why, once out of the priesthood, I felt free!

The attitude and mentality in a prison either makes or breaks a person. At Headingley, I became less sensitive to the comments and attitudes of others. A few officers, who offered me the opportunity to debrief with them during my transition, often asked, "Father Ray, will you be mentioning me in your book?"

I would smile and reply, "You'll be happier if I don't."

The transition was a time of things coming to a head, of identifying with differing points of views and spiritualities and of doing more meaningful work inside. As many people are rejected by society, I was rejected by the Catholic institution. But in the prison environment, outside of the church and surrounded by beautiful trees and nature, my relationship with God flourished... the prison set me free!

5
Reflections

My Spirituality

"He that planteth a tree is a servant of God, he provideth kindness for many generations, and faces that he hath not seen shall bless him."
— Henry Van Dyke

Spirituality is the vehicle we use to get closer to God. For many, the practice of religion feeds their spiritual life; for others, the practice of recreation, the arts, time in nature, time with a friend or a good book feeds their spirituality; and for still others, these practices complement the religious faith they cherish.

My spirituality used to be within a religious context that included words such as guilt, sinful, immoral, perverse, and not normal. These words had me living a life of ambiguity: with a God of unconditional love while being taught that what the Pope said, God said, and that I was going against God's plan of creation in being gay, and living a sinful life because of my sexuality and erotic fantasies.

In order to live a normal gay life with a God of unconditional love, I needed a spirituality outside the particular religious box that I had been born into.

Within the formal church, words such as obedience, penance, infallibility, celibacy, submission, abstinence, excommunication, annulment, and heresy, to name just a few, are needed to maintain power and control; eventually they became unacceptable to me. The language of faith, values, and beliefs is expressed in different ways by other religions and forms of spirituality and, for me, it is not and never was about which is better. It's about the need to respect, and to have the right to choose freely according to one's conscience.

My experiences have taught me that while maintaining steadfastness to my own path to truth, I need to respect all other paths to that same truth, which is that love is all, irrespective of religion, culture, colour or creed.

Just the notion of God conjures up all kinds of images and, for many, these images are quite negative. But many of us believe that God uses events and individuals in our lives to reach our hearts and to remind us to continue to have faith and hope. We blame God less by not using phrases such as "the will of God" or "an act of God". Instead we need only ask God to help us through the natural events in our lives.

The "spiritual revival" that has been taking place in recent years has offered me an image of God that is more believable, especially as a gay person. This image has helped me connect more easily with nature and with others who make up my life.

"He who knows himself knows God."
Hazrat Ali — Sufi

In 2005, I experienced a paradigm shift from an image of God as "father" to an image of God as "one divine energy, one infinite presence" outside a religious box — and for this, I owe eternal gratitude to my brother Gaetan. My brother always had a dislike for and rebelled against two institutions: school and church. For him, they were truly "necessary evils".

Unknown to me in 2005, Gaetan had been engrossed in the writings of Dr. Wayne W. Dyer, particularly his book *The Power of Intention*. So when he called me for information about the spiritual group that our younger sister belonged to, "The Army of Mary", he assumed that I, his religious brother, would be able to shed some light on Denise's very religious spirituality.

For our sister and her family, devotion to Mary brings them into a community of faith with strong spiritual friends, which enriches their lives and devotion to God. Though it is not a form of spirituality that Gaetan and I, nor our other sister, follow, it is one that we respect as being meaningful for Denise and her family.

So when Gaetan called to gain some insight from me, he was surprised to discover my own spiritual paradigm had shifted. As he spoke of his new-found spirituality, I was hearing a spiritual language that I could relate to, which was especially surprising coming from this unexpected messenger.

As I worked on moving forward throughout 2005 and 2006, Gaetan and I kept in close contact, giving each other spiritual support and encouragement. God does, indeed, work in mysterious ways.

There's a saying that when the student is ready, the masters appear and events are presented that open our minds to what we need. In July, 2006, while vacationing in Toronto, my friend Darren invited me to attend The Unity Church that he was attending at the time. The theme that Sunday was "Always look on the bright side of things" and, in keeping with that theme, though I don't think it was his intention, Darren was excited about introducing me to a book that he was reading, *You Can Heal Your Life,* by Louise L. Hay.

The following month, I was hired as a spiritual counsellor at a local health centre where I worked with four "alternative healers." I was so impressed with Hay's book that I began recommending it to my clients and using it as my own spiritual reading.

Within a few weeks, I saw the film *What the Bleep!? Down the Rabbit Hole,* which dealt with quantum physics. I was so surprised to hear others speak my spiritual language that I went back to see the film another four times that same weekend.

Then, from the Universe, Denise sent me the book and DVD called *The Secret,* about the law of attraction; I watched the DVD over and over again.

Shortly after that, she put the icing on the cake by mailing me Eckhart Tolle's book *A New Earth,* which deals with awakening to your life's purpose, which has the Oprah Winfrey imprimatur.

These spiritual writers led me to the language of my spirituality today, a spirituality in which I refer to God as Divine Energy, Infinite Presence. Others refer to the same God as Lord, Father, Abba, Allah, Krishna, Yahweh, Creator, Manitou, Higher Power, Mother Earth, etc.

For me, and many others, spirituality has become "being" in a harmonious relationship with myself — body, mind and spirit — as well as with others, and with God, whatever we might understand Him to be.

To have this harmony and balance within myself, I first need to be conscious of what is taking place in my life, in my body, mind and spirit in the "now", as Eckhart Tolle would say — and to be able to interpret, learn from, and be grateful for the experiences, no matter how difficult or challenging they may be.

When we are self-aware we are better able to connect to our conscience. We know something is right when our conscience is clear, which is why we need to learn to listen to and trust its voice. My conscience accepts my orientation and lifestyle as normal and fulfilling, whereas to a religious person, such a lifestyle might be seen as unnatural and perverse.

We must believe what our consciences and gut feelings tell us, and be responsible for our choices. Only then can we become the unique persons we are called to be, whether we are to live for a few or many years.

To have harmony and balance with others, we must have respect, love, tolerance, and honesty — in order to share our own truths while respecting the choices and beliefs of others, thereby drawing into our lives the people and events that our spirit-energy attracts.

On February 28, 2004, I saw a play entitled *Liar,* by Brian Drader, an actor, writer and dramatist who made Winnipeg his home at the time. I was able to relate to many statements he made in speaking about one of the main characters in the play.

I too, "had lived (almost) entirely outside of the box, and had defied conventional categorization."

I too, "could be all things..." (a good priest, a slut, a relative, and an acquaintance) "except possibly myself' (a compassionate, loving, gay male).

To most people who knew and worked with me, I too was "the mysterious stranger, the loner."

Brian also wrote that "intimacy and honesty need to be linked." When I finally realized the truth of that statement I began experiencing both honesty and intimacy. Indeed, as Brian said, "I found myself in a very different place," experiencing harmony and balance within myself, between my body, mind and spirit, and having learned a very different lesson — which was to let go and let God by living one day at a time — as prescribed in AA and other 12-step programs.

And to have harmony and balance with God, we are called to have daily gratitude and trust in the process of life, and to rest easy in knowing that our prayers are being answered by Infinite Intelligence. I believe that my spirit will continue in time to learn lessons from experiences, to become ready to be one with its source, its God.

Some, like Tom Bianchi, look for a language for happiness outside of the language of religion, of having the pieces but not the understanding needed to put them together. Having harmony and balance within ourselves and between ourselves and our Higher Power will bring about what many are searching for – happiness and inner peace.

Beyond reconciliation

$\mathcal{M}$y sister Carole, whose input and support has been a godsend, raised an important, though not surprising question: "Ray, why would God call you to be a priest knowing that you are gay?" Quite a loaded question!

A similar question is asked of married men who, after twenty, even forty years of marriage, "come out" — with all the shock and scandal that such an announcement always creates. But that same affirmation from a priest seems more sinister and deceitful to everyone — except for God and the priest himself!

However, while coming out was not a sinister and deceitful revelation to me, nor to God, in order to move on in my spiritual life and gain balance and harmony, I had some work to do:

1. ...on myself, because I had to accept that for my entire life, in keeping my secret to myself, I had not been honest.

2. ...on my relationships with others, because I had to address the whole difficult issue of reconciliation.

3. ...and on my relationship with God — I had to move my outlook and attitude to a place of gratitude for my journey.

1.　　From the beginning. I had not been honest with myself, nor encouraged to be. I was raised in a devout Roman Catholic home in which God was seen as "up" in heaven and was only happy with me when I was an obedient, good boy, like the one spoken of in *The Best Little Boy in the World* by John Reid, alias Andrew Tobias.

As a boy, I was very sensitive and knew early on that there was something different about me. Fearing rejection by my parents, I kept my secret with God.

As an adolescent, my emerging sexuality and attraction to males led to issues of acceptance and fear of being discovered — and a need for fantasies and masturbation. As well, I was filled with worry about my future and guilt for not being as good a boy as others thought I was.

Our parents were deeply concerned about each of their children, but our basic needs for love, affection, affirmation, and unconditional acceptance were experienced and interpreted differently by each of us. At the time, we were too young to understand what was happening and didn't have a language with which to articulate it at any rate.

As adults who survived the experience, we find ourselves almost estranged from one another, not having the closeness that we experienced as children. When we meet again, it will not be to hash over the past because our experiences of it were so different for each of us. Instead, it is my hope that we will meet each other in the moment, the "now", and move beyond any hope of reconciliation of past hurts.

Throughout my adult life, each personal crisis affected my physical well-being and, I believe, always had its roots in suppressing my sexuality. My body was trying to make me reflect on what was happening, to force me to make different choices in order to find peace and no longer feel so alone in the midst of so many people and so much activity. I was annoyed with authority, those to whom I had promised loyalty and obedience. I was searching for a place of belonging and my symptoms — anger, annoyance, and episodes of health problems — were my first sense of the price I would pay until I found that place.

During the transition to honesty with myself, I questioned every aspect of my life and identified with different points of view and spiritualities. Finally, I no longer saw rejection as negative, neither the church's rejection of me, nor my rejection of some of the beliefs for which it stood. The mini-transitions along the way were part of the process of letting go but still included intense emotion and loneliness.

In each transition, two things happened within me: I was told that it was no longer enough to be a priest and also gay; and I was offered an opportunity to clear the decks and be honest, particularly with myself.

In 1990, when my shrink asked me if I loved myself, I was dumfounded because it was difficult to love the image that others had of me, and which I somehow knew wasn't really me. I needed to be healthy within myself — body, mind and spirit — in order to take care of myself.

With low self-esteem, I had been living my life in survival mode, doing everything I could to meet the expectations of others; I was not thinking of self care.

At minor seminary, which was the beginning of my spiritual formation into the priesthood, I did gain a measure of acceptance and freedom as I became an adult and an individual with some sense of self. Being in the company of so many other men, it was also a time of homo-eroticism during which I felt, even more strongly, the need to protect my secret from others in order to remain accepted, even if it meant being dishonest with everyone.

Meanwhile, the Institute Voluntas Dei was giving me a spirituality through the 5-5-5, and through my walks in the woods, a new awareness that my relationship with God and a sense of God's presence could exist outside of the institution of the church.

Later, I began disliking some of the things I was asking of my parishioners because I no longer believed in what I was preaching. I was living with ambiguity but was not comfortable with the idea of accepting that ambiguity.

More recently, at a penitential service in which I was assisting a few priests in hearing individual confessions for a parish community, an elderly man sat in a chair facing me. He was obviously uncomfortable and quite upset about what he wanted to say. He told me that he was concerned about having masturbated a few times during the previous week. He was obviously sorry for committing what he perceived to be a serious sin when, in reality, he was deeply missing his wife, who had recently died.

His sad confession was one of the many experiences that finally brought me to the realization that I had had enough. I no longer wanted to listen to the guilt and shame that so many good people felt trapped within, particularly when I knew that by doing so I was enabling them to remain trapped.

At that same service, with a line of people waiting to confess such "sins" as having forgotten to say their morning or night prayers, or having missed mass, there was no time to reassure the widower that what he had been doing was not wrong, nor displeasing to God. In fact, I wondered whether I should congratulate him on still being sexually alive, or to merely forgive him for his "sinful" acts. I opted for forgiveness and asked God to forgive me.

I had often been reminded by bishops to keep my personal opinions to myself, to watch what I said and not cause waves. There were consequences for anyone expressing an opinion outside of company policy and without permission.

I met many wonderful people during my ministry and my greatest regret is not having been honest with them about myself. In the book *Intimacy,* Henri Nouwen writes that the more of us we deny, repress and stifle in a relationship, the more partial, limited and impoverished the relationship will be.

In every parish there must have been other men and women who carried the same secret as me, feeling they had to get married because, like Henri Nouwen and me, they feared rejection and the consequences of being openly gay or bisexual. Though I tried, my loneliness couldn't be alleviated by putting on clerical clothing; only through the company of others like myself, within a community in which I felt I belonged, could I hope for peace. What I didn't fully realize was the price I would have to pay for claiming my freedom.

I had always hoped that gay priests would be accepted by the church hierarchy but the expression, "Hell would freeze over first," applies here. In 2002, the silencing by the church of a priest and a nun, who were both involved in the gay movement, was a foreshadowing event for me.

With people in the gay community mentoring me, I was not only able to come out, but to burst out! My lifestyle was more open and obsessive. And then, having lived outside the box of dogmas, rules, regulations and labels, I came to understand and accept that I no longer could fit into communities that judged me.

I had invested a great deal of myself in my role as a priest — 25 years of my life. I lost many contacts and had to learn how to cope with the ensuing isolation and alienation, not only of leaving the priesthood, but also of preparing myself to be known as a gay person. This was the price to pay for "owning my truth", as Ellen DeGeneres calls it.

After spending so many years studying to become a priest, and having been encouraged to feel that I had chosen, and reached, the ultimate vocation, my experiences, social context, language, values, beliefs, faith, identity and energy were all within a very religious context. The Catholic Church invested a great deal of money and time to "form" me, and it didn't appreciate my stepping out of the program. A great deal time and energy was put into trying to keep me content and holding to the party line. And, indeed, I felt a sense of responsibility to Mother Church and to all who had helped me along the way; I didn't want to let them down. But when I did finally "step out of line", I had to either get reprogrammed or be honest with myself and move on. I moved on!

2.   Reconciliation with others has not been possible in every case, nor even of importance in some cases, though it certainly has been important in the process of my learning to own my truth. Many people have been significant in my life but I accept that it may not be possible for all of them to accept me for who I am, nor should they have to. But I am no longer alone; members of my current extended family all fly the same rainbow flag and do so with pride and gratitude to God.

I would like my sister Carole to know that I believe God spared my life in the 60s by leading me into the priesthood. Had I "come out" back then, rejection by our family and my friends might have caused me to take my own life or, entering the sexual promiscuity of that era, I most likely would have been among those who have since died of AIDS.

Though church institutions no longer meet my spiritual needs, I have moved beyond reconciliation to a spirituality and faith outside the institution. I have learned that, yes, God is certainly within institutions, but He is also beyond institutions and cannot be controlled, manipulated, nor copyrighted.

My meditations, Tai Chi, walks in the woods, and gay spirituality sharing groups have become my connection with God. With our God-given gifts and the spiritual and social support of whatever community we might belong to, God calls each of us to celebrate life with hope and pride.

I have always had a strong love of God, a caring spirit, and the creative flare and sense of humour that have kept me strong and likeable. God, the "One Divine Energy, One Infinite Presence, has used my gifts in the service of many.

Gay men and women are blessed by God with being born "double spirited". We are born to celebrate this gift in honesty and intimacy. But I believe men who are in committed relationships with women, yet frequent gay bath houses for physical intimacy, are seeking out others who have the same secret. No one, other than another kindred spirit, can understand this need, and only another kindred spirit who has had his secret disclosed, can understand with empathy the pain that his secret is causing, or will cause everyone in his life, especially himself.

Reconciliation with others, as much as it is possible, is also desirable. However, what is important is that each of us finds practices, whether religious or not, that express our spirituality, free our consciences, and allow us to be honest and intimate. I now see my spiritual journey, not as the price I have paid, but rather as the grace I have been given.

3.	Then there is my relationship with God. During the time between minor seminary and major seminary, I was an introvert, experiencing the world while still suppressing my sexuality, questioning my calling, and trying to figure out how God fit into my life.

During my pastoral experience in the Arctic, I felt God's presence in the wild nature of the north, just as I had found Him in the woods of the south. I gained a sense of freedom from authority in such life experiences while searching for a place in which I could be myself.

In major seminary, I was filled with anxiety and doubts around the notion of being "in" the world but not "of" the world. My relationship with God existed in rituals and I felt uncomfortable with church dictates that began with, "It is the will of God that...." or "God says..." In response, I always found myself thinking, *"Oh does he now?"*

Whenever I hear evangelists say "God told me" or "God told me to tell you," my mind tunes them out. I believe God does speak to us, and if God has something to tell me, He may do so through another person, but they won't be aware of it.

Identifying with causes and alternate spiritualities gave me freedom from the status quo of the church culture. But behind all my causes were the overriding issues of acceptance as a gay person, and how to relate to my place within the church. Through causes, my relationship with God was redefined outside the institution of the church as I became more honest in owning my own truth.

In order to move on and have harmony and balance in my relationship with my Higher Power, I accepted addressing God as Divine Energy, Infinite Presence.

I am now truly grateful for the gift of this journey that has been my life. It has led to my current spiritual beliefs and work as a spiritual counsellor, which offer me the opportunity of encouraging and creating wider acceptance and tolerance.

I am grateful for the relationships I have had with others because none of my life would have happened as it has without them. If not for the prison incident and the people involved, for example, I might still be a priest today, although, in the end. not really functioning as one.

My secret with God went on for years and accentuated feelings of being alone, but it also made me sensitive to issues of injustice within a minority group.

I am so grateful for the experience of feeling God's daily presence, and for the necessary lessons of faith and courage in my spiritual journey.

And I am extremely grateful to the Roman Catholic Church for the education it afforded me, for the formation of my spirituality, for the numerous beautiful people I have met and served, and the for the fraternity I have had with so many gifted and spiritual men and women. Though there may not be reconciliation with this community, which cannot accept me for who I am and how I live, I remain grateful; I have moved beyond reconciliation.

Conclusions

P ublic figures, such as James McGreevy, former New Jersey governor and author of *The Confession,* who had lived experiences similar to mine; Mark Tewksbury, Olympian gold medalist in swimming and author of *Inside Out;* and the entertaining TV host Ellen DeGeneres, have "come out" in support of gay rights as human rights. And although it might be fashionable to be a gay celebrity, it continues to take courage to be gay in mainstream society.

Throughout my years as a priest, I tried again and again to convince myself that if I tried hard enough to do things properly, according to what others expected, everything would be okay. I often felt there was no way out, that I needed to learn how to make the best of it. But I always ended up making waves and the cycle would begin again, starting with the feeling of being caged. Though many around me were kind and accommodating, they sensed that I was not happy but didn't understood why.

Maintaining my priestly lifestyle drained me of a great deal of energy and caused me to get physically ill about every five years. Shortly after being ordained, my body felt it had given up its freedom and vitality. I became a "tamed adult" and my body was drained of energy, of the real essence of life.

"Sexual energy is, in fact, spiritual energy,
which is the energy of the cosmos, which gives rise to life."
— Deepak Chopra

It often took all the energy I had just to cope with the petty accusations by parishioners or confrontations with a bishop. At those times, I felt ashamed, angry, sad, helpless, tired, confused, betrayed, hurt, stupid, frustrated, overwhelmed, lonely, fearful, and paranoid. But, along with the confusion, an internal awakening was always a part of my experience.

My last bishop saw that I didn't fit in and that I was a liability to him and his institution. By sending me to Southdown, his suspicions were confirmed, which justified his getting rid of me. That experience was not the tragedy I had feared it would be a year earlier. On the contrary, it was a catalyst in giving me the freedom for which I longed. I was able to ask my questions, to have my experiences validated, and to pursue my spiritual journey.

Some in the gay community say we need a gay God, but God created us to be who we are for the same reason some people are created black, white, yellow or red, or to live in Africa, South America, North America, Asia, or Europe. And that reason is so that our souls can have the experiences they need in order to grow closer to the Source, which is unconditional life.

For one soul, the "needed" experiences might mean being born in a Muslim body in Iraq or Montreal or California; for another, it may mean being born a fundamentalist Christian in the southern United States; for another, a young humanitarian with strong social and spiritual convictions and no religious affiliation.

The scenarios are as many as the humans on this planet. But what each of us has in common is that God created us to be compassionate and respectful of one another's differences and uniqueness.

"There is, I conceive, scarcely any tree that may not be advantageously used in the various combinations of form and colour."
Gilpin

I've heard it said that family is where our needs are met. As a gay male, I see our family's need to claim our God-given gifts and identity. Our gay directories are filled with the names of gay professionals who contribute to serving our health, legal, medical, social, and religious needs, and offer gay tourist accommodations and gay travel experiences. We have bookstores filled with every aspect of our gay rainbow.

Even television makes it fashionable to have someone gay in the script... but we have *always* been in them. Our human species is, indeed, becoming more tolerant, even though individuals, out of fear of their own sexual identity, continue to project their fears upon us.

Our sexuality, far from being a distancing, or distraction from God, is the instrument by which God creates us and manifests to us. People are blind to the holiness of the flesh by guilt, shame and fear, which is put on them by a patriarchal church hierarchy.

Being gay is God's gift of love, and our being loved by another is our way of experiencing God's love for us.

I read somewhere that without honouring our gay story, we cannot honour our God. Gay enlightenment comes, in part, from seeing the world from the perspective of an outsider.

Henri Nouwen struggled with the pain of the loneliness of keeping "the secret". He died from the burden of that loneliness, even while in the midst of a loving L'Arche community in Ontario, Canada.

In contrast, not long ago I ran into the youngest son of one of the families I had befriended as a parish priest. He was in his 30s then and, without talking about sexuality, my gaydar was aware of something we were not saying to each other. Then, during a subsequent Christmas visit with his family, he asked to speak to me about his secret. I envied his courage and ability to articulate his experience that day.

I'm now able to journey with him, to listen to his fears, anxieties and rejections. I encourage him to find gay support groups and to seek out professionals and spiritual leaders within our gay community to help him deal with the issues around coming out — or not — to family, friends and others in his professional life; and around whether to continue his religious faith in a community that doesn't accept him as being "normal", and judges his sexually active life as deviant.

This friend continues to have friends and business associates as a member of the larger heterosexual community, but now, when times get rough and lonely, he also has the gay community/family to reach out to for support and understanding.

Coming out can bring support and a renewed faith in God to move on in celebrating life, no longer lonely.

AFTERWORD

In 1994 an aboriginal elder gave me the title of Warrior of the Rainbow. In the aboriginal culture, the rainbow symbolizes different experiences and the passage from one world to another.

In 2006, that title again revealed itself to me when I was reading *The E-Myth Revisited*. In it, Michael Gerber quotes Don Juan in Tales of Power: "The basic difference between an ordinary man and a warrior is that a warrior takes everything as a challenge while an ordinary man takes everything either as a blessing or a curse."

The present moment can be challenging for us, but the challenge of living with HIV/AIDS, cancer, disability, rejection, loss, and a changing lifestyle can be the greatest help in our going beyond what has been, and not seeing our challenges as burdens.

My vision of the challenge for the Warrior of the Rainbow is to empower individuals to be themselves. I am a non-traditional thinker, approaching my work with passion. I help individuals to articulate their present life experiences and emotions in an atmosphere of non-judgment and respect. I work with people on understanding the three components of maintaining health: harmony within, harmony with others, and harmony with a higher power.

Warrior of the Rainbow affirms the faith and language of those who hold different views and beliefs and challenges people to respect others. My goal is to provide spiritual care to those who are grieving and to those who are seeking balance in their lives. It is my hope that this book, my story, the story about the making of a warrior of the rainbow, will help.

My spirituality is articulated by writers such as Louise L. Hay, Dr. Wayne Dyer, Eckhart Toole, and by philosophers, theologians and scientists who speak about quantum physics.

My spirituality is not a religion, rather it's about becoming consciously aware of the balance or harmony that is required within ourselves, between ourselves and with our higher power, whatever we understand that to be, in order to live one day at a time and to be in touch with what is most real in this present moment.

If there is no balance and no harmony. we will feel that we are just existing, trying to survive. If there is balance, we have positive and optimistic energy.

We are often preoccupied with relationships and resources. Our successes often bring more demands and expectations. Our achievements often leave us with wanting more out of life. We are often looking for something else, something we cannot define..

Within ourselves we are called to come to an acceptance of the present moment and be responsible for our choices. Between ourselves, we are called to have mutual respect; with our higher power, we are asked to understand that peace is in having no regrets and practising a daily habit of gratitude for everything and everyone who is a part of our spiritual journey.

There once was a woman who woke up one morning, looked in the mirror, and noticed she had only three hairs on her head.

"Well", she said, "I think I'll braid my hair today." So she did and she had a wonderful day.

The next day she woke up, looked in the mirror and saw that she had only two hairs on her head.

"H-M-M," she said, "I think I'll part my hair down the middle today." So she did and she had a grand day.

The next day she woke up, looked in the mirror and noticed she had only one hair on her head.

"Well", she said, "today I'm going to wear my hair in a ponytail." So she did and she had a fun, fun day.

The next day she woke up, looked in the mirror and noticed there wasn't a single hair on her head.

"YEA!", she exclaimed, "I don't have to fix my hair today!"

Printed in the United States
By Bookmasters